Inspired
By
Autism

Written by Claudreen Jackson
Inspired by Pervis Jackson, Jr.
Cover by Pervis Jackson, Jr.

ZOË LiFE
PUBLiSHiNG
WORDS TO LIVE BY

Published by:
Zoë Life Publishing
P.O. Box 871066
Canton, MI 48187 USA
www.zoelifepub.com

Medical Disclaimer

Please note that this book is for informational and inspirational purposes only. It is not intended as a substitute for informed medical advice. The user of this book should not use this information to diagnose or treat a health problem or disease without consulting with a qualified health care provider, specific tests, physicians, procedures, opinions, or other qualified medical information.

Author:	Claudreen Jackson
Cover Design:	Pervis Jackson, Jr. and the Zoë Life Publishing Creative Team
Editor:	Zoë Life Publishing Editorial Team

First U.S. Edition 2010, Perfect Bound Soft Cover

Publisher's Cataloging-In-Publication Data

Jackson, Claudreen

Inspired by Autism

Summary: Inspired by Autism is one mother's touching, brutally honest look at the depression, heartbreak, and frustration of a parent living with an autistic child—it is also an inspiring, heroic testament to the love and acceptance of a mother.

10 Digit ISBN 1-934363-59-6
13 Digit ISBN 978-1-934363-59-1

1. Autism, Parenting, Spinners, Pervis Jackson Sr., Celebrity, Motown, Faith, Hope, Caregiver of adult child with autism, Children with disabilities, Vaccines

Library of Congress Control Number: 2009927536

For current information about releases by Claudreen Jackson or other releases from Zoë Life Publishing, visit our website: http://www.zoelifepub.com

Printed in the United States of America

V11.1 1.2.10

Dedication

This book is dedicated to my husband Pervis Jackson, Sr. Pervis was a founding member of the Spinners, an award winning vocal group originally with Motown Records. Pervis was not only a star performer; he was a star human being. He mentored, supported and encouraged me as I was writing this book about our son, Pervis Jr. His inspiration helped shape the final product. Unfortunately, he died in August, 2008 so he did not live to see it.

Pervis is gone, but he will never be forgotten. The lessons, inspiration and motivation he gave me will go on and on.

Acknowledgements

Thanks to my older children, Cindy, Stephanie and Shawn for the years of support they have given me with PJ. Thanks to my parents Herbert and Grace Gilbert who are always available to take care of PJ. Because of my beautiful family, I've had a freedom that many parents of children with autism do not have. Thanks to my grandchildren who also make themselves available to help.

Thanks to Sabrina Adams, my publisher. Without Sabrina, there would have been no book. Thanks to the rest of my Zoë Life Publishing team who worked on this book.

Thanks also to the Spinners, star human beings who have continued to support and comfort me after my husband's death.

Thank you Pervis.

Thank you God.

To God Be The Glory!

Praise For
Inspired by Autism

"Almost any book that any parent has written about their kids with autism has portrayed it as something that is overcome by dedicated, smart and loving parents, leaving the impression that if the rest of us had tried as hard, our children would be 'cured' too. I am glad to read about the other side of the situation."

Dianne McClung,
Parent of a 33 year old son
who is handicapped by autism

"There are exceptions to every rule and the way The Jackson's accepted and focused on PJ's condition is the model of acceptance of challenge and turning it into a plus. *Rain Man* made increased public awareness of autism but *Inspired By Autism* shows what one can do when confronted by the situation and how to handle it."

Jonny Meadow
Peabody Award Winning Music Historian

"Claudreen is a very special person, who wrote a very special book, about a very special problem, in a very special way.

To be able to put your heart and feelings into print for someone else to read is a remarkable fete, but to be able do it and have the reader feel what you felt is truly incredible. This is what happened as I read this amazing book. I laughed, I cried and I was so completely mesmerized by each page that I could not put the book down for any length of time.

Long after I finished reading this piece of art, the events stayed with me. Only a truly dedicated person and loving mother could have gone through and survived such an ordeal. May God bless Claudreen and all the other parents who so gallantly give their hearts, minds and souls to the ones who need them the most."

Ruth Farley Sibert,
Retired Child Care Provider, Medical Assistant &
Fashion Show Coordinator

Inspired
By
Autism

Written by Claudreen Jackson
Inspired by Pervis Jackson, Jr.
Cover by Pervis Jackson, Jr.

Contents

Foreword 1

1. Before Autism..3
2. The Diagnosis...7
3. What About Me 17
4. A Child Called PJ 25
5. Living, Loving and Growing – I'm Coming Out..................45
6. I Can't Stand It 59
7. He Ain't Heavy, He's My Son.............................. 71
8. My Heroes..81
9. To Everything There Is A Season 95
10. Poetry Inspired By Autism................................ 99
11. Laughs Inspired By Autism 125

We Want to Hear From You 138
About The Author 139
When You Need Help the Most.....................................141

Foreword

Through her writing Claudreen Jackson allowed us an up close and personal look at the path she has walked with her son PJ. These writings reflect on the lessons she has learned along the way. It is amazing to me how strikingly similar our paths have been, as we move through this world of autism, she as a parent and I as an educator of this very special group of people.

Our paths first converged when PJ came into our lives at Burger School for Students with Autism. Over the years we were together trying as best we could to plan and predict what skills PJ would need in order to leave school and become an "adult" in his unique community.

Claudreen brought to us her son, she spoke of her dreams and wishes for his life. PJ shared with us, in his own way, the things he was passionate about. So school became the place where those dreams, wishes, and passions were the framework for our lessons.

The diagnosis of autism will influence each of us in different ways. Claudreen was able to accept it, to hate it, to love it, to cry about it, to embrace it and now to be inspired by it. She showed us through her gentle never faltering love for her son PJ that came first — then came his autism.

We are better teachers and parents for having worked with PJ because he is a very good instructor. In this blending of parent, teacher and student we learned from PJ the important lessons in life; to love the raindrops on our faces, to keep the music in our heart, and to color each of our days with the brightest crayons on the box.

Mary O'Neil, Ed.S.
Director
Burger School for Students with Autism
Garden City, MI 48135

Chapter One

Before Autism

*I*T WAS 1972. My husband belonged to a singing group that had just received their first gold record. What an exciting time! It was especially thrilling for me because I never thought it was going to happen. For years, the group had worked hard and struggled to get a hit record. They went to rehearsal every day and rehearsed for hours. They rehearsed at the recording studio on West Grand Blvd. in Detroit.

My husband's constant refrain was that, one day, they would have a hit record and I would not have to work. Since I don't believe in crushing people's dreams, I never told him that a hit record was never going to happen. My thought was that, one day, he would realize he was chasing a dream, wake up, and get a real job with a real salary.

They recorded with Detroit's preeminent record company at that time and produced a number of songs that did not make it to the top of the charts; it was disappointment after disappointment. How could he believe? How could he hold on, week after week, month after month? Was it ever going to happen? I couldn't understand this kind of endurance and perseverance.

They later left the record company and signed with a company in New York. Finally, they had the "hit" they had fantasized about for so long! My husband's dream was coming true and I was glad that I had kept my mouth shut.

Life became a whirlwind of TV shows, performances, out-of-town trips, press parties, celebrations, shopping sprees and sky's-the-limit opportunities to buy the things we had always needed and wanted — better furniture, better clothes and better cars. We had a lot to celebrate and would have a party at the drop of a hat. Our children were in high school and we had parties for the basketball team because they lost and needed cheering up. Then we had parties for the team because they won and wanted to have a good time. We had parties for performers who were appearing in town.

Friends would call and say they were coming by to visit. Next thing you know, other people would show up and a full-fledged party would be happening.

We attended the disc jockey convention in Philadelphia in 1972 (our first attendance at a major event since their record became a hit). They were appearing at a dinner for Sargent Shriver (father of Maria Shriver) who was the democratic nominee for vice president. We wives were told that we could not attend the performance because we had not been cleared by the Secret Service and the process would take days. We understood this because we had watched the secret service agents go over the area with a fine-tooth comb. They even checked under the ashtrays.

When an official from the record company found out that the wives could not attend the dinner, he went right to work to get us security clearance. In two hours, we had our pictures taken and were handed security badges so that we could be part of the event. WOW! I had never seen people accomplish so much in so little time. I felt so pampered.

I found my husband's success hard to believe, but he had always had the faith. I learned a valuable lesson about focusing on your dreams, working hard and believing it was going to come true. I would have given up, but giving up never occurred to him.

We were living the life! We were so exuberant about our good fortune that we decided to have another child. This would be the first child who was planned. This would be the first child that we could afford. We already had our baby sitters because the older children were all teenagers.

Who knew that along with success would come groupies and gropies who would be running all over me? Who knew that our planned for, much-loved baby was going to be the challenge of a lifetime? Who knew that by the time the baby was seven years-old, my husband and I would be separated? Who knew?

Chapter Two

The Diagnosis
Floundering In The Void

*P*J WAS BORN on July 1, 1975. He was a bright-eyed, curly haired baby who was always a joy. I was thrilled to be a mother again. His brother and sisters were excited to have a baby brother, and he was much loved and cared for by the whole family.

His first year was a normal first year. He hit all his developmental milestones right on time. He hardly ever cried and slept quietly most nights. He was a smiling, silent baby. If I was going to have another child in my mid-thirties, he was the perfect one.

On July 1, 1976, we celebrated his first birthday and I breathed a sigh of relief that I had birthed another healthy, normal child. (It was my last sigh of relief about him.) I took him to get his twelve-month vaccines, as I had done with my three older children and it was all downhill from there.

He started losing the gains he had made. He'd been saying a few words: "Hi," "Bye-bye," "Mama," "Daddy." He'd pass the stove and say "hot." I noticed a slight difference in his behavior, but I was not alarmed. He quit sleeping all night. He started crying all the time. He started throwing temper tantrums. He was no longer the happy, smiling child he had been. I thought he was going through the "terrible twos" early or that these were the things I would have expected in his first year and since he had been so good that year, I would accept his temporary change.

When he was sixteen months old, I took him back to his pediatrician for a follow up appointment. His pediatrician was a wonderful doctor who had a way with children. After a thorough examination of PJ, she gave him the Denver Developmental Test and I could see that he was not cooperating. But I was not prepared for what she told me afterward. During the test, he was jumping up and down and flapping his hands. He was throwing the testing objects on the floor. He would not sit in the chair, was constantly screaming and crying and was impossible to test. The doctor asked me if I was aware that he had regressed since last visit. (I was aware, but thought it was just a phase he was going through). She asked me if I was aware of the change in his behavior. (I was, but was hoping it was a phase). Maybe it was the "terrible twos" coming early. She said that judging by his behavior she thought he had autism.

In 1976, I had not heard of autism, but I knew that whatever it was I did not want it. I'd thought she was such a wonderful doctor, and now, because my son was having a bad day, she wanted to hang something serious and heavy on him. She must be wrong!

She gave me the name of a leading psychiatrist at Children's Hospital, located in Detroit's medical center area, and made an appointment for me to see him to confirm her diagnosis.

Surely, he would see that PJ was merely going through the "terrible twos" early and that there was not a serious problem. When I took PJ to see him and he confirmed her diagnosis, I thought, How can these excellent doctors be so wrong?

But PJ's negative behavior accelerated.

He was screaming all day and night; having tantrums on an hourly basis; hitting and scratching himself (and any of us who came close to him).

After three sleepless nights, I had to admit that maybe the doctors were right. I could no longer afford to be in denial because PJ was not only self destructive, he was destroying the house and me with it. I practically had to live in the bedroom with him in order to keep the house from being demolished.

Eventually, I began questioning whether or not I should have taken PJ for his vaccines. In case you're wondering why some parents of children with autism point to the vaccine as a cause, it is because we're aware that before the vaccine, we had a normal child, PJ included. I, too, believe that the vaccine has something to do with the cause of autism, but I believe it has something to do with how the vaccine is stored as much as what might be in the vaccine.

He had been given vaccines in 1975 as was the routine and all was well. However, after getting the measles, mumps, and rubella vaccine in 1976, I saw drastic change. The doctor had told me that he might become a little ill from the vaccine, so I was not concerned when he did become ill. At first, I attributed his behavior change to illness. Babies get cranky when they don't feel well. But his crankiness went on and on and on and on. His pleasant personality and progress never returned.

Though I am suspicious about these vaccines, I would never advocate discontinuing them. They were created for a reason and if we stopped giving them, we would have an even greater problem on our hands. I believe that we need to examine the ingredients and explore how and where it is stored.

I believe this because I saw a report on television about improperly stored vaccine that was used in 1976. The reporter said the children who had been vaccinated that year with that particular vaccine were being diagnosed with various medical conditions, including autism. This hit a nerve with me. I had been asking: "Why? Why? Why? Could this be why?"

I tried to contact the reporter. I tried to track the story down through the health department. I had no luck in either case and discovered that I was reaching a dead end. I was exhausted from dealing with PJ and decided that I had to use what little energy I had to try to mother him.

So I realized I had to accept the diagnosis, but I would find the cure. Isn't this America? Aren't we sending people to the moon? Don't we have the best of everything in America? I knew that we could fix autism. It was simply a matter of finding the right doctor or facility.

There is no medical test for autism. It is diagnosed through a checklist. The Autism Society of America, along with each state society provides the checklist. The checklist is also in the offices of pediatricians and child psychiatrists and special education departments. Any of them can send you the checklist, but I am providing it here. I went through the checklist to see what applied to PJ. I don't remember who gave it to me, but my heart got heavier and heavier as I read it.

- **No real fear of dangers.** ☑

  (If we were ever near a lake or river, PJ wanted to jump in. He was always trying to jump from high places such as balconies or railings that were put there to protect us.)

- **Apparent insensitivity to pain.** ☑
  (He was self abusive.)
- **May not want cuddling.** ☑
  (He didn't even want to be touched.)
- **Sustained unusual or repetitive play.** ☑
  (He would fill containers with water and pour water for hours. He would tear pages from the phone book and line them up on the floor.)
- **Uneven physical or verbal skills.** ☑
  (He made a lot of noise and many sounds, but none with the intent to communicate. He was extremely physical, trying to climb drapes and always standing on tables and counters, no matter what was already there.)
- **May avoid eye contact.** ☑
  (If you tried to cuddle or make eye contact, he would hit you.)
- **May prefer to be alone.** ☑
  (He was always pushing us away.)
- **Difficulty in expressing needs. May use gestures.** ☑
  (If he wanted something, he took you to it and put your hand on it.)
- **Inappropriate attachment to objects.**
  (He did not like toys, but he loved the boxes they came in.)
- **Insistence on sameness.** ☑
  (You could not move furniture. He often broke things, trying to move furniture back to its original place.)

- **Inappropriate response or no response to sound.** ☑
  (He appeared not to hear well, but we knew his hearing was good.)
- **Spins objects or self.** ☑
  (He was always spinning around in circles.)
- **Difficulty in interacting with others.** ☑
  (There was no interaction.)
- **Inappropriate laughing or giggling.** ☑
  (On the rare times that he laughed it was very inappropriate.)
- **Echoes words or phrases.** ☐
  (Since he does not talk, he does not echo)

In the months that followed, I sought out a round of doctors and facilities that I thought were better equipped to handle autism than I was. I went from doctor to doctor, in hopes of finding the one who would accept PJ for treatment.

Every doctor told me that there was no cure for autism. In fact, one said, "He is not only autistic, he's mentally retarded. You see what he's doing now? That's what he'll always be doing."

What PJ was doing was jumping and flapping and saying "Ge, Ge, Ge." I asked these doctors to recommend a facility for him – they couldn't, and I had a hard time accepting this.

When I returned from one of these visits, I would sink more and more into a depression. What was going to become of him? What was going to become of me? What I didn't know was that the year that PJ was born (1975) was the year that the federal government started actively breaking down the big state institutions. Funding for mental health was tied to whether the states were closing their institutions. Doctors could no longer suggest that clients be institutionalized.

I felt like I was living in the "Twilight Zone." I could not manage his behavior and I could not find any professional who would take him on. In fact, I could see the looks on the doctors's faces when PJ and I arrived. They were not happy to see us.

I was tired of making the rounds. I was exhausted from the lack of sleep. I had no sense of direction about this child. I was confounded and could find no meaningful help or guidance. I was crying everyday and going to bed in the middle of the afternoon, usually for the balance of the day. One day, I cried, "Lord, nobody wants to take my son." A little voice said: "Not even you." What a revelation! If I did not want him, who would?

This revelation pushed me even further into a depression. Was I actually going to have to figure out how to mother this impossible child myself?

The little voice said: "Well, you are his mother."

"Yes, I'm his mother but this was not the child I had expected. This was not the child I had looked forward to. This was not the child that I had in that first year."

Have you heard the changeling story? The story goes that the fairies or elves come and steal your baby and leave one of their own. I felt that the author of that story must have been writing about a child with autism. I felt like my smiling, happy baby had been exchanged for this new, little person who I did not know.

My Depression

People do not like to know when you are depressed, so I did not tell anyone. Remember all the parties and traveling I was doing when PJ came along? Well, I had everyone thinking that I was still traveling with my husband and too busy to attend certain events. When friends called, I would inform them that I was on my way to the airport for an extended trip. One day, when the phone rang, I thought, "I can't force myself to try to have a conversation with another person." I sat there, too tired to move. The phone stopped ringing, and I decided not to answer it anymore. I couldn't keep talking and pretending that everything was all right.

What to do about this child? For one thing, the doctors told me I would have to keep him "centered." How? No one told me how to keep him centered. I was giving him medication, but sometimes it didn't work and we had to try something else. I realized that I wasn't centered myself. How could I center myself? Would wine help?

He was still climbing drapes, walking on counters and tables, and screaming constantly. Since he did not like to be touched, there were days that I did not even try to dress him. There were days that I did not dress myself. There were days that I did not even get out of bed.

When I did get out of bed, if he was in a bad mood, which was all the time, I might get knocked off my feet. Although he was small, he was strong. He would tackle me from behind and down I would go. He would always catch me off guard. How could such a little person be so angry?

I was sinking deeper and deeper into depression. I realized that I was not doing anything except crying and staying in bed. I wasn't getting dressed. I wasn't cooking; I wasn't cleaning; I wasn't even combing my hair. Everything required too much energy and too much thought; even normal everyday things. I realized that I was on the verge of a nervous breakdown. "Good," I thought, "I'll have this breakdown and I won't have to worry about autism anymore."

I surveyed a bedroom in shambles – my bedroom. PJ had completely destroyed it.

Drapes were on the floor because he had been trying to climb them and they could not hold his weight. He'd cleared everything off the dressers so he could walk on them and that was all on the floor. He had torn pages out of the phone book and they were on the floor. I thought about how embarrassed I would be if someone had to come into the bedroom to remove me after my breakdown.

I'd better clean this room first, I thought. After I was finished cleaning the room, I realized that I needed to take a shower and wash my hair. I needed to buy groceries so the children would have food while I was gone. I needed to wash and iron some clothes for PJ because I did not want his sisters to have that to do. It took me three days to set things right.

I was ready for my breakdown, but it didn't come. Should I go turn myself in? Turn myself in where? What do people do when they have a breakdown?

A couple of years later, I was able to tell this to a psychiatrist I was sitting next to at a meeting. I told him how badly I needed him during that time. He said that I had worked my way through it. He said that instead of a breakdown, I'd had a breakthrough. That was a relief!

Later when I read "The Renewing Power of Your Mind" he referred to a nervous breakdown as the big NBD. He said that at some point, people would give up and give themselves permission to have the big NBD. I remember when I thought I would welcome the big NBD. Maybe it's good that my house was such a mess.

3

Chapter Three

What About Me?

About God

Like a ship that's tossed and driven
and battered by an angry sea
When the storms of life are raging
and the fury falls on me
I wonder just what I have done that makes
my race so hard to run
Then I say to my soul, "Don't worry.
The Lord will make a way somehow."

I USED TO SING "The Lord will make a way, somehow" to myself when I was poor and could not make ends meet. Now, I was no longer poor, but I still had reason to sing that song. I had a recording of it that I listened to over and over.

I have learned that if God gives you a problem, He can give you what you need to handle the problem. If you are in the dark, He can turn on lights for you so that you can find your way. If you are weak, He can strengthen you. If you are down, He can lift you up. If you have faith as the grain of a mustard seed, He will answer your prayers, but I did not always feel this way.

In the beginning, I was very upset with God for saddling me with such a burden. This child was impossible and I was not prepared for this. Wasn't I a good person who tried to follow His commandments? Why was He punishing me like this? They say that God never gives you a greater burden than you can handle. I took issue with God about this because I knew that I could not handle this situation. I was an abused mother. I was living in a "Twilight Zone"; in a situation that I would never have imagined.

I was constantly asking God: "Why me? Why me? Why me?"

They say you're not supposed to question God, but I believe that since He created us, He knows that there will be questions.

I knew that there was no cure for autism, but I felt that God could cure PJ. I prayed, begged and entreated God to cure my son. I had sought the help of numerous physicians, and had always been sent home with the same answer: There is no cure for autism.

"What do you want from me? God, what am I supposed to do with this child?" The answer from God was that He wanted me to accept the person He had given me. This was not what I wanted. I wanted a cure! We can do everything else in America. Why can't we cure autism? (Remember, this was in the late 1970s.)

On one of my visits to PJ's school, I again questioned God: "Why did You even make people like this? What are they good for?"

The answer from God was that He made people like PJ to make people like me better. Wasn't I a kind, gentle person? Didn't I always have a kind word, a hand out or a helping hand for people who needed it? Here was this little person right under my nose who needed my help and I was rejecting him.

One day, after PJ had, once again, knocked me off my feet, I really let God have it. I refused to get up off the floor and asked God if this was what He had in mind for me when He created me. I railed at God for doing this to me. I was very disrespectful to God.

The next day, I was horrified at the things I had said to God. I begged for forgiveness.

"Can you please, please forgive me?" I asked over and over.

I was heartsick.

A friend of my daughter's dropped by unexpectedly. She didn't know that I was avoiding people. I had to let her in. I can't remember our short conversation, but during the course of our conversation, she mentioned that God always forgives us if we ask forgiveness. That was my answer! God forgave me, but I decided never to be that disrespectful again.

One day, while PJ was having what I referred to as an explosion, but the doctors termed an "episode," I could see how miserable he was. His face was pure misery. I felt so sorry for him that I quit feeling sorry for myself. Like the story of Pinocchio, he finally became a real little boy. God had not cured PJ, but He had cured me.

"OK God," I said, "I'll try to be his mother, but I don't have the wisdom or the strength. I need Your help. I'm turning PJ over to You." Have you heard the song, "Take your Burdens to The Lord, Leave Them There?" I decided that was what I had to do. Give my burdens to the Lord. I gave PJ birth, but it was God who gave him life so PJ was entitled to his little space on this planet just like the rest of us. I quit apologizing for his existence.

My daily prayer was:

Precious Lord, take my hand.
Lead me on, let me stand.
I am tired, I am weak, I am worn.
Through the storm, through the night
Lead me on to the light.
Take my hand, Precious Lord, lead me on.

Books started coming my way. Another parent of a child with autism gave me the little booklet "Thought Conditioners" by Norman Vincent Peale. She said it helped her greatly and it also helped me. I read it over and over. A friend gave me "The Greatest Miracle in the World" by Og Mandino, about rescuing ourselves from the scrap heap of humanity. I read "The Renewing Power of Your Mind," a book that said the mind has an infinite capacity to renew itself. Was this true? Could my overwhelmed mind renew itself?

In the last chapter of this book, there's a list of the books I read to renew my mind and spirit. If I was going to mother PJ, I needed to try to get myself together. Lord knows I had plenty of time to read and reading does not take any energy.

The Bible verses that helped me greatly were: "*Come unto Me, all ye that labor and are heavy laden, and I will give you rest*" (Matthew 11:28); "*Be ye transformed by the renewing of your mind*" (Romans 12:2); "*I can do all things through Christ which strengtheneth me*" (Philippians 4:13); and "*They that wait on the Lord shall renew their strength; they shall mount up with wings as eagles; they shall run and not be weary; and they shall walk and not faint*" (Isaiah 40:31).

Of course, there are many more verses that helped me, but these are some of my favorites.

The fifth chapter of Matthew and the third chapter of Ecclesiastes were always uplifting to me, as well as the Gospel songs I mentioned earlier in this chapter.

I had been paralyzed by fear, afraid to make a move in any direction. I read II Timothy 1:7 every day:

"For God has not given us the spirit of fear; but of power, and of love, and of a sound mind."

Dr. Norman Vincent Peale said, "There is only one force more powerful than fear, and that is faith. When fear comes to our mind, counter it with an affirmation of faith." I'd had a great fear of what was going to become of PJ in the future. I decided that I would be his future, so I would not have to worry about his future. (I still worried about mine.)

I'd always had faith, but now I needed greater faith. If you know the outcome of a situation is going to be positive, then you don't need faith. Faith is the belief that things will turn out all right in spite of all evidence to the contrary. Faith is the belief in things hoped for but not seen. I had faith that God was going to help me mother PJ and was going to help me take care of him. Have you heard of "Stepping out on faith?" I stepped out on faith many times during my journey with PJ. The faith has to come first before the hoped for outcome. My faith was always justified. The following story is an example:

PJ love to eat French fries. Though he cannot talk, he has always had ways of letting me know what he wants . When he wanted fries, he used to bring me the bag of frozen fries to cook for him, sometimes two or three times a day. I became concerned about him eating so many fries, because he did not have a balanced diet. One day, I saw a magazine article entitled, "Foods That Help People With Autism." I bought the magazine and decided that whatever the foods were, I was going to buy them.

The article said that some foods increased the serotonin level in the brain and this made people with autism feel and act better. One food was pasta. Another was potatoes. No wonder he ate so many fries! It made him feel better. As a result, I felt better about cooking so many fries for him. I cooked fries for him so often that it became automatic and I became careless.

One day, as I was heating oil for his fries, I became distracted in another room and forgot that the oil was heating. When I returned to the kitchen, the pan was on fire. A normal child would have been alarmed and told his mother. (This is an example of him not recognizing danger.) I thought that I could move the pan just a few feet to the sink. Even though I had a pot-holder, the pan was too hot and I dropped it. A wall of flame erupted.

I ran to get PJ. He is bigger and stronger than me, and cannot be moved unless he wants to move. He can't be forced to do things. He has to be influenced, prompted and guided. I did not have time for that.

To my surprise, he ran out of the side door. I'd thought that I'd have to save him, but he saved himself. He did recognize the danger!

I was thankful that we'd gotten out, but I was so scared. What about all the damage to the kitchen? I would have to go to a neighbor's house to call the fire department. I thought I would peek back into the kitchen to see how bad it was. Looking through the window, I did not see any fire.

Cautiously entering the house, I still did not see any fire. Not only was there no fire, but once I cleaned up the spill, the floor was not even scorched. Nor was the wall. There was no evidence of a fire at all!

God had taken care of me and PJ. That was the only way to explain what had happened. "Except ye see signs and wonders, ye will not believe!" (John 4:48)

We now cook fries in an electric deep fryer. PJ has learned to cook his own fries and he never leaves the kitchen. He hovers around watching until they are just the way he wants them. Then, he carefully removes them, just the way he has seen me remove them.

I learned my lesson. I remain in the kitchen when I am cooking.

Chapter Four

A Child Called PJ

PJ WAS SUPPOSED to be my easy child. I already had three older children, so this one would have the benefit of getting a mother with experience. I needed to remember this experience because in the 60s and 70s some doctors had said that autism was caused by cold, refrigerator mothers. The theory was that since the child was normal at birth, the mother had rejected the child and caused the autism. I had to remind myself that I had not caused autism in my other children, so I knew that theory was wrong.

My older children provided the assistance that allowed me to keep PJ at home. They were my back-up when I needed it, which was often. My oldest daughter, Cindy, was instrumental in my acceptance of PJ.

During my years of depression (following the diagnosis), Cindy could not stand seeing the pathetic person I had become. This was that awkward period when I was lying to friends, telling them I was busy so they would think that I did not have time for them. I was hiding out in my bedroom, but I had my friends thinking I was traveling extensively.

I could not hide out from my children. Cindy would say: "You need to comb your hair" or "Are you going to put on clothes today?"

She was always on my case. She bought me a book, "A Child Called Noah," and told me I needed to read it.

"OK, Cindy, I'll read the book," I said.

An hour later, she came back. "Have you started the book?"

"Not yet, but I am going to," I said.

After three or four of these exchanges, Cindy sat down and started reading the book to me.

The book was about a child called Noah who had the same kinds of behaviors as PJ. I'd thought I was the only parent who'd gone through this kind of situation. I finished reading the book on my own because it was a revelation to me.

Cindy brought me other books to read. I called it "Cindy's required reading" because she would check and ask questions to make sure I was reading them. I began to see that other parents had found a way to live with a child like PJ. I needed to know that I was not alone in my struggles with a difficult child.

Years later, when I asked her how she knew just what books to bring me, she said she would ask the librarian or bookstore clerk for advice. She would describe the situation to them and they would recommend a book. Cindy confided in me that she wanted the mother that she knew back.

I decided to search for just the right haven for PJ. That would be my solution. Then I could go back to being the person

I used to be. Except, the law had changed in 1975 and because of that no doctor would refer PJ to an institution. I made the rounds, looking for the ideal place for him. Why did they think that the only place for him was with me? Why did they keep sending me back home with him?

I constantly cried that I was not prepared for a child like this. Now, I realized that I had to prepare myself for the fact that I was going to have to keep him.

Lafayette Clinic was one of the residential, mental health facilities in Detroit. I made an appointment to take him there because I'd heard that they were an excellent treatment facility. I already knew that they would not keep him there, but I was hoping for outpatient treatment or referrals. There was no outpatient treatment for people with autism. There were no referrals. Another brick wall!

Despite my disappointment, I did meet a doctor at Lafayette Clinic who helped me a great deal. Although she could not help PJ, she helped me by listening to me and giving me sympathy. Lord, I sure needed sympathy! She scheduled an EEG test for him. According to the test, his brain waves were normal, so that was not an area in which he needed assistance. On another visit, she had PJ videotaped, then gave me an appointment so that we could watch the video together.

I did not like looking at PJ extensively because I could not stand his bizarre behavior, but as I watched the tape with her, I learned to observe his behavior objectively so that I could learn ways to deal with it. She pointed out that he had "object permanence," and good powers of reasoning and logic. Additionally, she pointed out his actions on the tape that had caused her to come to these conclusions. At last, a doctor was giving me some tips I could use!

I also discovered that parents of children with severe disabilities went through stages. The first stage was denial: "not my child" or "this is a temporary situation." Thinking it was temporary was easy when it comes to autism because they are so "normal" that first year or two. The next stage was bargaining: If my child is cured, this will happen or I will do thus and so. Another stage was grief: You had to grieve for the child you thought you had before you could accept the child that you actually had. The last stage is acceptance of your child, whatever the deficits. You have to reach acceptance in order to move forward. I felt that I had been going through grief long enough. I would have to work on acceptance.

Around this time, I saw a public service announcement on TV. In the announcement, a phone number was provided to families who suspected their infant or toddler had a developmental problem. Because my situation was far beyond "suspecting," I called the number. The number was for Project Find, an early intervention department of the Detroit Public Schools. Project Find was established to assist the parents of children who had been struggling with developmental challenges since birth. PJ was three years old.

The staff at Project Find got right to work. After interviewing me and meeting PJ, they enrolled him in a diagnostic prescriptive school. Prior to this meeting, I had no idea that such a school existed. PJ attended that school for three weeks for observation. He was picked up in the mornings in a cab and brought back home in the afternoon. He had what was referred to as "curb to curb" service. Everyone seemed to genuinely care, including the cab drivers.

Next, he was offered additional observation and diagnosis at a school for children with disabilities and learning challenges. My relief at finally getting help was short lived because the school could not keep him. After a week, the staff told me he could no longer come back. All the children there had problems and PJ was adding to their problems by attacking them. I was afraid that PJ would hurt one of the other children. I agreed with the staff that he was too aggressive.

We had also enrolled PJ in nursery school. He attended nursery school in the afternoons. The head of the school was a teacher we knew who said that she would accept PJ. She had experience with children with problems and felt that she could help him. However, PJ's unruly behavior was more than she anticipated. Just like the previous teachers, she had to let him go in order to protect the other students. He was three years old and already had been kicked out of two schools!

We'd been trying different medications to control his behavior but could not always get him to take the medicine. He seemed to think pills were poison, so we would crush the pills and hide them in jelly, peanut butter, or applesauce. There was always a big fight to get him to take his medicine and it would take all of us together to accomplish this.

Then, one day, his older brother, Shawn, simply handed him the pills, and PJ quietly took them. He finally realized that they made him feel better. He has been taking his medication with no problems since then. In fact, if you forget one, he will bring the medicine to you. Of course I prefer liquids, but they don't all come in liquid form. He chews the pills because he cannot swallow them whole and drinks his favorite juice afterward.

Next, he was enrolled in a classroom for emotionally impaired children. I sat down with his new teacher to go over his Individualized Educational Program (IEP). She went over her goals and objectives for him. I wondered how long it would take for her to give up, too. The doctors had already told me nothing could be done in his case, but she seemed to think that she could accomplish these goals and objectives, such as toilet training, less disruptive behavior, following simple instructions, etc. so I did not tell her what the doctors said. Everyday, I expected the call to come get him.

That call never came.

Not only was she working with PJ, she was accomplishing her goals. I was amazed. He was being toilet trained. At first, I had to send three pair of training pants each day. Then it was down to two; then one; then none. He was using the bathroom. What a relief that was!

When we had our next meeting, I saw scratches on her arm. They looked just like the scratches on my arm. I tried not to ask, but I had to know.

"Did PJ put those scratches on your arm?" I asked.

"Yes, but that's OK, he's learning better behavior," she said, shrugging it off.

"Doesn't he hit you?"

"Yes, but he's so little."

"What do you do when he hits you?" I asked.

"I turn to the other side and say, you have to hit this side, too"

"Doesn't he throw things on the floor?"

"Yes, but I make him pick them up."

"How do you make him pick them up?"

"I put his hand on whatever he has thrown on the floor and move his hand to the table to put it back."

"You are so calm with the students. How can you remain so calm?" I said.

(I was always yelling in panic at PJ to stop something he was doing or I was yelling "Oh, no" at something that he had already done.)

"I don't yell because I want them to know that if I raise my voice, it's for a reason, such as danger."

That made a lot of sense to me, so I decided to keep my voice calm when talking to PJ at home. He responded so much better to my "calm voice" than my "yelling voice." What a lesson for me! Home was becoming more peaceful.

At Christmas time, she wanted to take the class to Cobo Hall to see the beautiful Christmas decorations and she needed parents to help. I didn't think PJ would care about or notice the decorations, but I reluctantly went in order to support her and to help with his behavior.

When we were at the Christmas Carnival, I saw more children with disabilities than I had ever seen at one time. Students in wheelchairs, on crutches, with helmets, and all kinds of disabilities. Why are there so many children with disabilities here today? Then it dawned on me that the children are why we were there that day. This was special needs day.

I realized that each one of these children had a parent who was struggling with their child's disability. God Bless these parents! God Bless these children! I also realized that I was glad that I did not have a child who was medically fragile, or one who needed a nurse at all times. These parents had to make frequent trips to the hospital in order to save their child's life. At least, I did not have that concern. Maybe some parents had it worse than me.

Without even trying, this teacher taught me as much as she taught PJ. As I watched her and marveled at her methods, I saw that she was optimistic about the progress of her students. I saw that some of her optimism worked and was rubbing off on me. The doctors had said that he could not be cured. She did not promise a cure, but we could move him from Point A to Point B or C. We could not go from A to Z, but we would move him along as far as we could.

I finally realized that my goal for PJ should be the same goal that I had for my other children – to develop whatever potential he had and to see that he had a good quality of life.

This was the goal for us parents whose children could not be cured. A cure was not in our power, but the power we did have was to see to it that they had a good quality of life.

During those days when PJ was being transported to the school by cab, something unusual happened. The cab pulled up; the driver opened the door, and this little boy got out. He came into the house, took off his coat, and went to the refrigerator to get a glass of juice (the same routine that PJ had), only this wasn't PJ!

I ran to catch the cab driver to let him know this was the wrong child. PJ was quietly sitting in the cab while my new little boy was drinking a glass of juice. We made the exchange, but this was an example of people with autism not being aware of their environment.

PJ remained in this classroom for three years before going to another teacher. Now he had a male teacher. I was glad about this because there are so few male teachers in elementary school. This teacher, along with a social worker, made a home visit to observe his activities and behavior. They were surprised to see how many "normal" things he did at home. I was always impressed with DPS staff and their willingness to make house calls.

These classrooms were for students with emotional impairments. When PJ was seven, he was transferred to a school for children with autism, Burger Developmental Learning Program. At that time, the incidence of autism was so rare that there was only one autism program for the over 30 school districts in Wayne County. I'd thought that autism was going to decrease instead of increase. However, it has increased and the other districts eventually had to develop programs for children with autism.

Because of his aggressive behavior, I was comfortable placing PJ in a school for children with autism, but many parents of children with autism wanted their children to be mainstreamed into a regular education classroom. Burger was considered a "segregated facility" and at one point nearly closed it doors for good. In another example of parents speaking up for their children, so many parents protested the closing that the school remained open.

I loved his teachers at Burger. I felt that they were just as caring as his teachers in Detroit had been. His teacher even gave me her home phone number in case I needed to talk. I appreciated this so much. In fact, it had impact on my future in the classroom. Years later when I started teaching, I gave my phone number to the parents of my students as well. I was very impressed with all the teachers who worked with children with autism because I knew, first hand, how difficult they are to teach. Some are very resistant to learning, as was PJ.

The Burger staff got PJ involved in Special Olympics, because he was very physical. He won quite a few gold medals for running and jumping. The first time he won a gold medal he came home, removed the medal from his neck, and dropped it in the trash. I retrieved the medal and told him that this was something important that we wanted to keep.

He is an excellent skater as well as a fast runner and loved these sports. Winning a medal meant nothing to him. He participated for the sheer joy of the sport. (I never got involved in sports because I knew I would never win. I wish I had participated for the joy of participating, but us normal people want to win, or at least not be embarrassed).

We enrolled him in an ice skating program for people with disabilities. Although he had never ice skated in his life, he took off on the ice skates as if he had been ice skating forever. The program was in the suburbs and PJ was the fastest, loudest, biggest, blackest student in the program, so he became well known. You could not miss him. People began to cheer for him at the skating competitions.

At one competition, PJ was distracted by people cheering. He missed one of the cones and was disqualified from first place. He finished the race and had to take the third place medal. When they gave out the medals, PJ was supposed to remain on the third place podium, but he was so used to first place, that he climbed to the first place podium and stood there along with the first place winner. They both stood there smiling! (We know that would not have been the way "normal" athletes would handle that situation.)

Until I became the parent of a child with a disability, I was not aware of all the disability rights organizations in the state of Michigan. One of the primary goals of all the organizations is for people with disabilities to be included in community activities. I agreed with these goals and though I did not like taking him very many places because his behavior was unpredictable, I began taking him to the store and to the park and other places where we could make a quick getaway if necessary. Also, now that he was taking his medication, his behavior was more manageable.

Although we were separated, PJ Sr. decided to take us to Disneyland, where the group would be appearing. We had planned to celebrate PJ's seventh birthday there. The only problem was that he would be coming from another engagement, so PJ and I were supposed to meet him at the airport in Los Angeles. We scheduled our flights so that PJ and I would be arriving about a half hour before his father.

I'd been so concerned about how PJ would act on the plane that I had almost backed out. I knew that once we got to LA, I would have his father's help, so that gave me the courage to proceed as planned. PJ was very good on the flight because he slept all the way.

When we went to pick up our luggage, I found out that his father's flight would be delayed over two hours. I was stuck at the airport with PJ because I didn't know the name of the hotel where we were going to stay. It was midnight and every place that I could have called to get information was closed. This was also before the days of the cell phone.

PJ's behavior began to deteriorate. He became loud and aggressive. We were getting a lot of attention. I was so embarrassed by his behavior that I did not sit down and wait, but I kept moving from place to place, so as not to be too disruptive to the other people. I also had our luggage with us, so by the time PJ Sr. did arrive, I was exhausted, my nerves were frayed and PJ was totally disruptive. "Why did I do this?" I thought. "I should have known better."

Later after both of us had a good night's sleep and PJ had taken his medication, I felt better and so did PJ. One of PJ Sr.'s singing partners said to PJ Jr., "I'm glad to see you in a good mood, Jr. because you were as evil as a bear last night." The other members of the group always treated PJ just like they treated everyone else.

PJ loved Disneyland and his behavior greatly improved. I even saw autism drop away at times. We had pictures taken with the characters, including the bears from Bear Country. I loved this, but PJ was not too happy with these characters.

The show that his father was in was called the "Rolling River Revue," and was one of the best shows I have ever seen. There were beautifully costumed performers dancing and singing on rafts that moved down the river. There was a showboat with dancers that moved down the river. PJ Sr.'s group performed on an island in the river. There were huge American flags unfurling and fireworks. PJ and I were both mesmerized. Autism was not an issue because during all this PJ was almost as normal as the rest of us. Now I was really glad I'd had the courage to come.

PJ has been to Disneyworld a number of times. He loves Disneyworld and Disneyland as do I. I also love seeing him become almost normal during these trips. Talking is still a problem, but Disneyworld is the only thing he will talk about.

Other than bowling, skating and Disneyworld, he is interested in music (of course). He plays his own tapes and listens to music for hours. He also has a beautiful singing voice, but he only sings the part of the songs that he likes, mostly humming, with a few words thrown in. He seems to play a tape in his head until he gets to his favorite part then starts to sing. We had him sing with his sister at an autism benefit. This was for autism, so whatever PJ did would be all right or so I thought. PJ sang with his back to the audience. Oh well.

He likes grocery shopping. For years I did not take him to the grocery store because he wanted to open everything then and there. He was not good at waiting in line either. We've had a few scenes and tantrums in grocery stores where I wanted the floor to open up and swallow me.

Once he learned to wait until we got home to open things and learned to wait in line, we started grocery shopping again. He buys all his favorite foods, French fries, sausage patties, chips, etc. He also buys things he has seen on commercials, which is why I ended up with Maxi-pads after I no longer had use for them. I also switched my laundry detergent to his choice because of commercials he had seen.

He loves eggnog and would always get it during the holiday season. After the season ended, he bought buttermilk thinking it was eggnog. And there followed another scene when he found out it was not what he wanted. I taught him to read the words on the carton and he has not made that mistake again.

When PJ was seven years old, my first granddaughter, Jacinta, was born. PJ loved the baby and would say "baby" when he wanted to hold her. He was very careful with her, smiling like a proud parent. The problem came when he was tired of holding her. We were always there because he would just let her go.

He gave her eye contact, which the rest of us did not get. She was the first person that he ever kissed. I watched him start to give her a kiss, then pull back, over and over again. Finally he really kissed her, but it was difficult for him that first time. When she got older, she also did her part in trying to make him normal. She was always giving him instructions and guidance. He never got angry with her as he did the rest of us when we were telling him what to do.

He loved to give Jacinta eye contact. He would hold her face in his hands and she would let him look into her eyes as long as he wanted. On one visit, she left her doll behind. PJ would carry the doll around and look into the eyes. I don't know how it happened, but one day, he had just the head of the doll in his hands. He carried the head around looking into the eyes.

PJ and I lived in disorganized, tenuous harmony for a few years until he reached puberty. He started having seizures and became aggressive again. Now he was bigger than I was and I could no longer physically control his behavior. Once again, I started trying to find the appropriate facility for him. It had to be the right place. I did not find that place and I had struggled with him for so long and he had come so far that I did not have the heart or energy to continue searching.

His brother, sisters, and I did an intervention by restraining him and talking to him. We had to show him that there were limits to his behavior and that he could be controlled. This was one of the times that I relied on his powers of reasoning and logic. He seemed relieved to be controlled and his behavior improved enough that I decided to continue keeping him at home. My original decision had been that I would keep him at home as long as I could.

When he was fifteen, I prayed for him to have some age appropriate behaviors. My prayers were answered. He became interested in cars and girls. The only problem was that the girls he became interested in were the same age as my granddaughter who was seven at the time. All he wanted was eye-contact, but I had to keep him from approaching little girls. My granddaughter helped the situation by giving him all the eye contact he wanted when she was visiting. We also let him look into the doll's eyes again.

Another habit of PJ's was his setting off the car alarm trying to open the door. He pushed my small car out of the driveway more than once. We were blessed that no other cars were coming along at these times. I finally had to sit in the car with him everyday and let him turn the steering wheel to get it out of his system. After that, I quit telling God what I wanted PJ to do. I have faith that God will take care of us the way He always has.

My faith that we will be taken care of has gotten me into some unpredictable situations. On one occasion, his father was performing at Pine Knob, a local outdoor amphitheater in Michigan. PJ Sr. would be performing so I was on my own with PJ. I wasn't worried because it was outdoors and I knew we could go backstage if necessary.

PJ and I were sitting in the audience. I was wearing a hat because I was having a bad hair day. At one point, I was standing up at the same time that the band played a note that hurt PJ's ears. He pushed me, I fell back into my seat and my hat rolled down the aisle. So there I was, bad hair and all trying to catch the hat before it rolled too far away. What a sight! (One of the times that PJ and I were a sideshow.) I've often said that I never knew whether we were a tragedy, a comedy, or a sideshow. I still don't know.

I do know that I am younger, healthier and stronger than I would have been if not for PJ. This fact inspires me to keep him, even when the going gets rough, as it did a few years ago during the time that I was teaching.

I would come home from work to find him upset and disruptive. After a full day of teaching, I needed to come home to peace and quiet. Finding a place to put him again became a goal, but we were able to make an adjustment in his medication so he calmed down and I decided once again to keep him at home.

The latest behavior that had me concerned was his leaving the house by himself, which he'd never done before. I'd decided that we should take a neighborhood walk two or three times a week. Big mistake. He was no longer afraid to leave the house on his own. Of course, being autistic, he was walking out barefoot, in pajamas or, sometimes at night.

I was in bed one night when I thought I heard the door open. PJ had taken a shower, put his pajamas on and gone to bed. I attributed normal ways of thinking to him, so I thought maybe I was hearing things and he was in bed. Then, remembering that he has autism, I checked his bedroom. He was gone and the side door was wide open. I had to put on a robe and shoes to try to find him. If I could not find him, I would have to call the police. We lived on a divided street where the median is an area of grass and trees. You can only go one way on either side of this median which is called an island. This makes the street much wider. PJ was on the other side of the street, across the island, barefoot and in pajamas.

I made him come home and tried to get the point across that he should not leave the house. This didn't work, and he kept walking out when he felt like it, any time of day or night. He was slick enough to wait until I was in the bathroom or bedroom. (I thought people with autism were not sneaky.) I had to start keeping a closer eye on him and one day when he left, I followed him. He was moving fast, down the street, around the corner, across another street while the light was red.

I had a new doorbell installed, one that rings whenever the door is opened. The next time that he tried to sneak out and the doorbell rang, he hurriedly closed the door with a lot of shame on his face. He no longer tries to sneak out. He knew exactly what he was doing.

He now attends a day program for adults with autism. I've found that even though he is an adult, he cannot be left to his own devices. He still needs a structured environment. Some people still do not like programs specifically for people with autism, but autism is such a unique condition that I am comfortable with PJ being in what is referred to as a "segregated" program.

One day, when I was visiting the program, one of the differences was plain to see. There were about fifteen tables and about fifteen clients. When they picked up their lunch trays, they each went to a separate table. The average person would have joined someone else at a table in order to socialize. They had no desire to socialize, which becomes a problem when they are included in other programs. Do we force socialization on the ones who do not enjoy it? PJ rebels if too much socialization is forced on him.

I saw another difference at programs and dances at the day program and at the Burger Alumni Night gatherings. The young men would dance with another male as well as with a female. It seemed to make no difference to them. One of the young men wanted to dance with PJ. He would come and stand by our table and wait for PJ to get up and dance with him.

Since the diagnoses of autism has increased greatly – unless they find a cure – we will be needing more day programs because there will be more adults with autism in the community. Currently, there are a number of helpful speech and behavior therapies available for children with autism. The problem is that these treatments are very expensive and time consuming and many parents cannot afford them.

We are also registered with the Goodwill Agency that oversees our situation. PJ has a doctor and social worker who have all his pertinent information. In addition, he has an Individualized Treatment Program (ITP) that we created together. I have faith that I will be healthy and strong for years to come, but in case I am wrong, they can step in and finally find a place to put him.

I've said that PJ is not cured of autism, but he is far more advanced than when he was younger. He is no longer that wild, uncivilized person he used to be. He has far more self control and knows that he cannot hit people when the situation is not to his liking or when his routine is disrupted. The older he gets, the easier he is to live with. In the beginning, I'd always said that I had to adjust to him because he could not adjust to me, but he has learned to adjust to me and others.

That is why he has lived at home so much longer than I would have thought possible. I've not yet had to find a place to put him. When I used to talk to my cousin about finding a place to put him, she said: "You have found a place to put him – you put him in your heart."

5

Chapter Five

Living, Loving and Growing – I'm Coming Out

MY HUSBAND'S GROUP was experiencing great success, but I could not enjoy it. I was bogged down in autism. The groupies and groupies were running over me. My husband was running over me. PJ was running over me. I did not have the strength or energy to get out of bed most days.

I knew that I had to do something. The only situation that I could change was the chaotic relationship between my husband and me. Our marriage was as broken as my spirit and my nerves. We separated, and I moved into my own house with PJ.

Now that we were in a quiet, peaceful environment, I realized that I needed even more peace and quiet because it was good for my nerves. I turned off radios, TVs and telephones. I would sit on the couch and appreciate the silence and pray. The silence felt so good that I would sit for hours.

Lo and behold, PJ started joining me! We would just sit there together in silence. I discovered that he needed the silence and peace just as much as I did. These times were great because while we were sitting quietly, I did not have to worry about his destructive behavior. I did not have to try to control him. I could feel my nerves getting better.

I had been so angry with my husband (PJ Sr.) that I never wanted to see him again. I needed to recover from our relationship, but we had PJ and I knew that I needed his father's help, so I tried to keep our relationship on a positive level. (I was not always successful with this goal.)

For three years after we separated, PJ Sr. took care of all our expenses at my house. He paid the mortgage, utilities and bought us groceries. He took PJ shopping for clothes and to the barber shop. He took him skating and to the park. PJ was our common ground and we both wanted what was best for him. PJ Sr. made sure I always had spending money and was always there if I needed something for PJ. Though I knew that we could not live together, I had to admit that my husband was not all that bad.

He took me on trips when they were performing. (When we were together and I would ask to go on a trip with him, the answer was usually no.) I decided not to hold that against him because I needed breaks from PJ. I finally got to attend the Grammy Awards after I had given up on going to that event. I got to go to some islands in the Caribbean that I had always wanted to visit. The hot sun, warm water and palm trees were just what I needed. Of course, I always had to come back home to PJ.

Now that I was feeling better and his father was taking care of our expenses, I decided I would work on curing PJ. I read everything I could about autism. (Much less information was available then than now). I tried to mirror PJ; I tried to resonate with PJ; I tried to find a professional who would work with PJ. I wasted a lot of time and money taking him to speech therapy. Not only does he not really want to talk, he has aphasia, a speech impediment that he would have to overcome. He was extremely aggressive and uncooperative during these sessions, but I had to try.

There were two techniques that were popular during his childhood that I wanted to explore: Auditory Integration Training and Facilitated Communication. But I was not able to try them.

Auditory Integration Training was a technique of putting headphones on the person with autism and playing various sounds that were supposed to help their brain waves.

Facilitated Communication was a technique that required another individual to support the autistic person's elbow so that the autistic person could type out his thoughts. There were reports that this technique worked well with many persons with autism. I tried this with PJ, but was never able to get him to type his own thoughts. He only typed words that I gave him on flash cards.

(I have included my contact information in the back of this book. If you're a parent who has tried these techniques, please get in touch and let me know what you think about them.)

I thought PJ was going to be cured because God was on our side. But sometimes when we ask God for something, the answer is "No," the same way that we, as parents, sometimes have to say no to our children. I don't know if God said no to me, but I realized that the brick wall of autism was not going to come tumbling down in our case. They talk about the "window" of opportunity to cure autism. With PJ, I could not find the window or a crack in the wall. I felt that God wanted me to accept this person just as he was.

I wondered if I could love him even if he were not cured. I wasn't sure.

Have you heard of *acting as if*?

Sometimes I had to act "as if" I loved him because he wasn't being very lovable at that time. I would "fake it until I could make it" because I read somewhere, when people are the most unlovable that is when they need love the most. My love for him depended on whether I was feeling sorry for myself that day or feeling sorry for him.

I read what Og Mandino said about love in "The Greatest Miracle in The World:" "Love is a gift on which no return is demanded. To love for fulfillment, satisfaction, or pride is no love. Love that is not reciprocated will flow back to you and soften and purify your heart." I now know that this is true, but then, I was just trying to be a mother to a child I thought would never love me back.

I actually felt as if I was just five minutes short of me becoming autistic myself. That's when I realized he was not going to be cured and that I had to give up on trying to cure him.

I was telling this to a school social worker from Detroit Public Schools who was making a house call. I told her that I was tired of being depressed, tired of crying about autism and needed to find something to take my mind off my troubles.

Thanks to her, I had hope. Instead of staying in the house with PJ, I began traversing the state in my quest to find the person who would help me find a cure.

The school social worker had put me in touch with Dr. Ingrid Draper, who was in charge of the Special Education Department for Detroit Public Schools. Dr. Draper had a Parents Advisory Committee and asked me to join. I joined the committee, but I was not expecting her to really take the advice of parents. I was wrong! When she asked parents for advice, she acted on our advice. She really cared. The Special Education Department was at its best when Dr. Draper was in charge.

Dr. Draper started a conference for parents and teachers of special education students called "Special Connection." At our meetings, she asked parents and teachers what they would like to see done. Three parents made requests; one parent wanted information on guardianship; another wanted information on self-esteem; I wanted lessons in stress management.

To my surprise, she gave us just what we asked for. That class in stress management taught me how to manage my considerable anxiety. The fact that she listened to us and really cared about what we wanted was a revelation. Being with other parents of children with disabilities was also informative.

They had the courage, commitment and dedication to make a better life for their child. This was something that I needed to see and be a part of. I learned a lot from these parents. I learned to speak for my child, since he could not speak for himself. I'd been traveling among the "Beautiful People" in the world of entertainment. I was meeting another kind of "Beautiful People" – parents and professionals who were making life better for children with disabilities.

It was at one of the Special Connection Conferences that I heard something that gave me chills. Our keynote speaker encouraged us parents to continue speaking up for our children. He said that in the early days, students with disabilities were not allowed into the classroom. They were tied to a big revolving wheel in the schoolyard and the other students would throw rocks at them. What a horror that was to me! How far we had come!

I also became a member of the Michigan Society for Autistic Citizens (MSAC), which is now Autism Society of Michigan (ASM). The executive director at that time was William Walsh. He started asking me to go to meetings of various agencies, and to tell them of my experiences with autism.

I was intimidated because most of these meetings were with professionals in various capacities, such as doctors and executive directors. Bill Walsh told me just to say what was on my mind and what I had been going through. He refused to allow me to remain intimidated. He would not give me any advice about what to say, so I learned to speak for myself (and more importantly), for PJ.

When I'd been trying to find a support group for autism, I could not find one. There's a support group for everything else, why not autism? It added to the feeling of living in the "Twilight Zone."

I had not been successful because MSAC was located in Ann Arbor and I had been looking in Detroit. That meant that I would have to drive to Ann Arbor to attend meetings. At that time for me, it was a daunting forty mile drive, but being with other parents of children handicapped by autism was something I needed. I was learning from them. (Now parents can go to the Internet to get information and communicate with other parents).

MSAC had asked our legislators to give autism its own category because autism was included in the mental retardation category. Although some individuals with autism also have retardation (PJ included) they are distinctly different disabilities.

The legislators had turned down the first request and now we were going back to speak to them while they were in session. This time, they honored our request and autism received its own category. I learned something about the legislative process in this country: Enough people making the same reasonable request using the proper procedure can make a difference. I also learned that, if at once you don't succeed, try, try again. This is America and ordinary citizens are allowed to speak their minds.

MSAC was dedicated to making life better for people with autism and keeping them in the community. MSAC sent groups of parents and professionals to study with Dr. John McGee at the University of Nebraska in Omaha. Dr. McGee had written a book entitled "Gentle Teaching" about working with people with aggressive, challenging psychiatric disorders.

I was one of the parents lucky enough to go. I say lucky because I so agreed with Dr. McGee's methods that it was an honor to meet and learn from him. He said that when you are dealing with these people, you have to "define your posture" ahead of time. That meant that you would not change your behavior because they became difficult or aggressive. As their caregiver, your responsibility is to remain gentle. You could work on changing their behavior through the tasks that you gave them. He gave us techniques to use to accomplish this. You accepted the persons where they were and tried to lead them to where you wanted them to be.

The more I learned about treatment of people with disabilities, the more afraid I was that if PJ was not living with me, he would be somewhere in restraints or overly medicated. I felt that I had to keep him with me to make sure he was well taken care of because he was so disruptive and aggressive.

I recalled a movie I'd seen about autism: They showed a room in an institution that was filled with people with autism. They were humming, spinning, and flapping, each in their own world. Aggressive ones were in restraints. This is what happens if you leave them alone – nothing. This also gave me chills and inspired me to continue advocating for people with autism.

I talked to parents of adults with autism or retardation. They told me about how they were treated in the big state institutions. The inmates were lined against the wall, naked and hosed down (this is how they were bathed).

Dr. Draper and Bill Walsh had gotten me started, and I continued by joining other disability rights organizations. If I wanted a better world for people with disabilities, I had to do my part. I had to speak for my son because he could not speak for himself. I had to see what was going on in our state for people with disabilities. I did not have a lot of goals myself, but I was committed to offering my perspective and helping parents who had goals that I admired.

I was appointed by Governor James Blanchard and later, Governor John Engler to the Michigan State planning Council for Developmental Disabilities (the DD council). This was an advisory council to the governor. It was composed of people with disabilities, parents of people with disabilities, and agencies that provided services to people with disabilities. I was thankful that our governors cared enough to solicit our advice.

I really hadn't thought about people with disabilities until PJ came along. The DD Council said that we are all only one accident or one illness away from a disability ourselves. With modern medical technology saving the lives of more people, there are more people with disabilities. Indeed, a "developmental disability" is simply a disability that a person is born with rather than one that is acquired through an accident or illness.

I remember that when I was a little girl, once a person was confined to a wheelchair, they could never leave their house. Today, with ramps, lifts, and other alternatives, there are more places in the community that are wheelchair accessible. They are no longer forced to remain at home. We never know who among us will one day need these services.

MSAC had to go through an annual review process with United Foundation (now United Way). We were one of the agencies funded by them. Each year, UF met with the agencies they funded to determine how the money was being used. Bill Walsh would have me attend the agency review to testify, along with other members of MSAC.

I also became a member of the United Foundation Speakers Bureau. We spoke to companies who donated to UF to explain how their donations were utilized. I liked getting out to tell my story but also to say "thank you" and explain how much I appreciated them for their donations. I even received an award one year for helping to increase donations.

These activities were great at helping me to rebuild a self-esteem that had been shattered by the failure of my marriage and by my inability to find the answers I was looking for to help my son. I was also able to meet parents and experts who had been dealing with autism longer than I had. I could ask questions and share my thoughts and feelings. One autism expert told me that I was just as much an expert as he was because I was living with autism. He was interested in how I handled specific situations and he and I had a great conversation and exchange of experiences.

Of course, there was always PJ waiting for me at home. He had no clue of what I was going through on his behalf. Nor could he see a situation from another person's perspective, or understand how another person felt. I was still battling depression, but decided never to let fear paralyze me again.

I thought about how I'd used to have a sense of humor. I realized that it had been a long time since I had laughed a real laugh – nothing in my life was "funny" anymore.

I decided to start watching situation comedies to see if I would find anything amusing.

"The Cosby Show" and "The Golden Girls" did not disappoint me. I would always get a good laugh. I would get a glass of wine (considered as food in some countries), sit down and watch these shows and pretend that autism didn't exist. This was also during the time of the "Mork and Mindy" show. Mindy's method became one of my keys for dealing with my son. I figured that if he were someone from another planet, I would try to teach him Earth ways, right? So that's what I decided to do.

When PJ was ten years old and I was forty-five, I decided to see if I could handle a semester of college. I'd take classes while PJ was in school. I didn't think I could go to college long enough to get a degree, but maybe I could handle one semester. A little more college would also help me feel less intimidated by the meetings I was attending.

The University of Detroit is one of the best colleges in the state and it was also just two minutes from my house. I went there to investigate enrollment. I was assigned a counselor who was encouraging and helpful. She looked at my grades from my Associate's degree and began my educational plan. It did not occur to her that I might be attending for only one semester, so I said nothing about that.

Given my home situation, college was extremely difficult. I took it class by class, semester by semester, never being sure whether or not I would be able to finish. None of the professors said, "We'll take it easy on you because you have a son with autism and you are over the age of forty-five." (This is what I wanted to hear, because I sure told them my situation.)

During one semester, I was approached by the Office of Campus Ministry to be a conversation partner. I said yes, primarily because I assumed my partner would be someone I could commiserate with – I'd tell him or her my troubles and he or she would share in return. Boy, was I wrong. Being a conversation partner meant interaction with an international student. In other words, an exchange student was going to practice speaking English with me. In addition, I was expected to help the student learn about American customs. I was assigned an over-forty graduate student from China. He spoke very little English and of course, I spoke no Chinese. Our first meetings were a mixture of pictures and gestures to communicate. (How did I get myself into another "Twilight Zone" situation?)

Eventually, he became the answer to my prayers for evening classes. He became my boarder which meant I had a sitter for PJ. PJ Sr. would stay with PJ sometimes, but he was still traveling extensively. Therefore, I hadn't signed up for classes at night. All that changed when my conversation partner moved in.

He rented the basement but he would stay upstairs with PJ while I was in class. His instructions were to not give PJ any instructions, so that PJ would remain calm. My boarder would tape his classes, translate them to Chinese and then do his homework. I really admired his hard work and perseverance. If he could take classes with the language hardship, I could take them with the PJ hardship.

My boarder was not intimidated by PJ's behavior. In fact, he was interested in the relationship between PJ and me. He translated an article I had written about us into Chinese. He sent the article to his wife in China and she got it published in a magazine. She eventually moved to America, too. The two of them gave me a new appreciation of all the advantages we have in America that we take for granted.

I graduated with a Bachelors degree in 1989 and started teaching in Detroit Public Schools in the Special Education Department. Dr. Draper was still the director of the department and I was greatly honored to become a teacher in the Detroit Public Schools.

I taught students with learning disabilities and I loved my students. I loved the fact that I could teach them without encountering the brick wall I so often faced with autism. When I was teaching a lesson and they got it, I was overjoyed because I knew I was helping prepare them for the future. I appreciated the fact that they could communicate ideas and express what was on their mind. I was getting the feedback from them that I did not get from PJ.

I was so thankful for special education because it helped me greatly with PJ and I wanted to give back, but now, it seems that we are losing some of the gains we made in special education.

Chapter Six

I Can't Stand It

THERE HAVE BEEN many things that PJ does that I just can't stand.

When my older children lived at home, I would get dressed and leave the house after a day of dealing with PJ especially when it got to the point that I could not stand it any longer. I would leave him for his brother and sisters to deal with. (They were not always happy about this, but I knew they would look after him.) They told me that they would pass him around to each other when they could no longer tolerate his behavior. In the course of a day, he would wear us all out. I don't know how parents of children with autism make it without others in the household. You have to have help.

He used to jump up and down, flapping his hands and saying "Ge, Ge, Ge." After an overdose of this behavior, I would get to the point that I could not stand it a second longer. I would get his hands and hold them down to his sides to stop him.

Around this time, I read a book called "Son Rise" by Barry Kaufman. He described how his family had brought their son out of autism. He said that one of their techniques was to mirror their son's behavior so that they could "resonate" with him. I decided if they could do it, I could too.

The next time that PJ started jumping and flapping, I did too. I said, "Why are we doing this PJ?" To my surprise, he did not like to see this behavior in me any more than I liked to see it in him. He stopped jumping and flapping and grabbed my hands and held them against my sides. He soon stopped jumping and flapping.

He used to scream all the time, day and night. Once, I got to the point that I could not stand it a second longer. I thought, "If he screams one more time, so will I." He did and I did! He did and I did! We had a real scream fest for a while.

I had read about a psychiatric theory called the "primal scream therapy." It said that if you had a scream inside you, you had to let it out. Although I based my screaming on this therapy, and I was resonating with PJ, after we calmed down, I was quite embarrassed. "No one will ever know this," I thought, "because I'm never going to tell it."

When my daughter, Stephanie, came home from work that day, she called upstairs to me with alarm in her voice.

"Mom, are you all right? Are you all right?"

"Yes, I'm all right. Why do you ask?"

The children in the neighborhood said that they heard a lot of screaming from this house and they thought someone was killing you." So much for my secret, but after that PJ quit screaming so much. He did not like seeing my autistic behavior any more than I liked seeing his.

I also could not stand the fact that he was self-abusive. One day, he was on the floor, screaming and hitting his head against the floor. I found myself leaning against the wall hitting my hands on the wall and crying. It dawned on me that I was doing the same thing that he was, only in a more normal way. Why was I doing this? Because I was overwhelmed, upset, and frustrated. Could that be why he was acting that way?

I decided that I would have to be the "normal" one in this situation. I could not behave the same way he did. But, how could I avoid being upset when he behaved like this? I decided that I needed to walk out of the room and remove myself. I would go to the kitchen, get a glass of wine and try to ignore his behavior.

When I walked out of the room, so did he. He got up off the floor and followed me into the kitchen. I'd thought that he was so much into his autism that he would not notice what I did. I was wrong! This made me see how I might have inadvertently fed into his autistic behavior.

I couldn't stand taking him out in public.

He was not aware of any change in his environment and behaved the same way in public that he did at home, so we always attracted a lot of attention and a lot of comments. He looks so normal that people did not realize what a serious situation I was dealing with. I used to wish that the ground would open and swallow us. I often tried to explain his condition, but back then, most people had not heard of autism and thought, "That's a terrible mother."

People would say things like: "Why can't you control your

child?" "If that were my child I'd straighten him out." "He needs a good whipping" and on and on, while my heart was sinking more and more.

I only took him out when it was absolutely necessary. On one visit to the doctor's office, we put on quite a show. He was furious because he had gotten a shot. So, he was pushing and hitting me while I was trying to make his next appointment.

He had an internal volcano that was always exploding, especially when something happened that he did not like; and boy, he did not like what had just happened. Children were lined up, staring at us. "My mother would not let me act like that, I'd get a whipping." "What's wrong with him?" I could not get out of there fast enough.

PJ would explode in public no matter where we were. He did not care how much my dress cost or if it was a designer outfit. He would pull my clothes so hard that they would sometimes tear. I resorted to flat shoes and pants when I was with him. Once, he pulled all the clothes in my closet down and broke the rod they were hanging on.

After awhile, I refused to go out in public even without PJ. I was losing my social skills because there was nothing on my mind but autism. I could get dressed up and go to an event or party, but I would be miserable. It was too hard to smile and try to make conversation.

I had not been getting respite. I'd felt that no one else could handle this type of behavior and I was afraid that he would hurt someone. I knew that, for my own sanity, I had to start getting some rest. I had to have faith that trained workers would take good care of him. Eunice Kennedy Shriver, who had started Special Olympics had also started respite programs.

There was a program available and, in spite of my misgivings, I applied.

The application process was daunting. Pages and pages of forms to fill out. A physical exam. Medication forms for the doctor to fill out. An interview. I knew why all of this was necessary, but it was a draining procedure and I was so exhausted that just getting through the application process was overwhelming. I gave up the first time I decided to apply for respite, but this time I knew that I had to follow through.

The medications had to be effective before you could turn a child over to respite workers. Because he had no concept of time, he had to have medication to sleep at night. Without it, he would be awake all night, running all over the house, clearing the tables and counters and screaming. However, we had finally found a combination of medications that helped keep his behavior under control. That gave me the confidence and the courage to turn him over to respite workers.

Prior to PJ, I had been of the opinion that medication was overused and did not want to rely on it, but I gradually began to realize that it was created for a purpose. It was the people who had abused medication that caused it to get a bad reputation. I had to realize that I was in a situation that I could not handle. And nor could anyone else without the aid of medication.

At one point, I told PJ's doctor, "You have to medicate him or me." I was worn and weary and my nerves were shot. His doctor knew what I was going through and gave me a prescription for medicine for my nerves. Respite and nerve medication helped me a great deal with the situation then and still does today.

One night, before the medication, I was sitting on the side of the bed with my head in my hands, crying "why me?" PJ had hit me on the head with a coffee mug. He hit me so hard that I saw stars, and I hit him back before I realized it. He fell against the wall. Now I was crying and apologizing for being such a terrible mother. PJ came at me again and caught me with an uppercut that had me seeing stars again. So much for me feeling bad about hitting him.

Situations like this made me know that since respite was available, I needed to get it. Respite for caregivers is necessary, though I'm not sure that there are enough programs available. Respite programs are similar to group homes except they are used for short periods of time so the parent can have a break from the responsibility of caring for their child. Please let me know about your experiences in this area.

Another avenue for respite is camp. I did not want PJ to go to camp because, at that time, there was only one camp that took children who had autism and it was so far away that I was uneasy about sending him. At least, the respite facility was closer. The executive director of MSAC, Bill Walsh, encouraged me to send PJ to camp. He assured me that PJ would be well cared for and I decided that, in spite of my misgivings, I would try it.

The first time that I took him to camp, he seemed okay at first. Once he realized that I was going to leave him there, he started screaming and holding onto me for dear life. He had to be pulled away from me. Leaving him that far away was so difficult that I almost changed my mind. The camp was in Michigan's Irish Hills and his screams were echoing in my ears as I drove away. I was crying and praying. I turned him over to God.

I know that God is everywhere, but I prayed to God to remain with PJ instead of with me if necessary. I had faith that God would take care of him. Still, I did not enjoy the time that he was away because I was so worried. I kept expecting to get that "You have to come get him" phone call. Now I know how to make the most of my respite time and to enjoy it.

When I went to pick him up after camp session was over, I saw a different little boy. He was calm and smiling and even seemed to stand taller. Being out in nature with trees and water had done him a world of good. The camp counselors said he had not given them any trouble. He has gone to camp most years since then.

A couple of years later, a friend of mine was hired to be a cook for a camp for people with disabilities. Any disability except autism, that is. The camp had no experience with campers with autism and did not want to take a chance. This was not the first time that I had experienced a program for people with disabilities that would not take people with autism. It was common practice then. I hope things have changed now with the increase of people diagnosed with autism. Let me know. Autism was considered an "orphan" disability and I sure felt like it.

The camp directors did say that PJ could attend one of the sessions if I came with him as his counselor, so off we went. I love nature and water too, so I felt it might be good for both of us. We both needed the healing properties of outdoor activities and nature. I feel like we see God's fingerprints in

His creations of water, trees, mountains, etc. I actually feel closer to God when I am outdoors in a beautiful setting.

One day, the camp staff took us out on the lake on a pontoon boat for an activity. We both thoroughly enjoyed the boat ride. The next day, while everyone else was at lunch, PJ wanted to go for a boat ride. We did not eat meals with the rest of the campers, so we always had the whole camp to ourselves during those periods.

PJ was crying and pulling me toward the water. He was even saying the words "boat" and "water." It is such a surprise when he says any words that I try to respond by encouraging him to say more words (it hasn't worked, though).

I walked down to the shore of the lake with PJ with the intention of going out in one of the paddle boats. Common sense returned, and I realized how dangerous that would be. Everyone was at lunch and no one would be around if something happened to us. Neither of us knew how to swim, PJ was unpredictable, and we were an accident waiting to happen.

What should I do? We were at the water's edge and PJ was excited about going on a boat ride. There was a canoe there, and I decided that we would sit in the canoe until I figured out what to do next. PJ and I climbed into the canoe and sat on the shore and looked at the water. I could see him calming down. We sat for about a half hour before we got out of the canoe and walked away. Sitting in a boat, looking at the water was just as effective for him as actually going for a boat ride. Who knew it would work out like that?

I thought that once he got over those bad habits that I could not stand, we would live in peace and harmony. I was wrong! He still does irritating things such as: pouring out dishwashing liquid, laundry detergent, and bleach.

When I saw how interested he was in these products, I decided to teach him the appropriate use for them. We measured the appropriate amounts to use in the laundry or dishwasher, and I let him be in charge of pouring. Little did I know that as soon as my back was turned, he would empty the containers. He ruined washers full of colored clothes by pouring the whole bottle of bleach into them. So now, I hide these things so they will be available when I need them. Sometimes he finds them and pours them out. Sometimes I forget where I hide them.

I can't stand it when he runs the washing machine or dishwasher with nothing in them, one of the results of my teaching him how to use them.

I can't stand it when he throws away perfectly good food. Once, after I had cooked fries for him twice and he had thrown them away, I went on strike. I would not cook any more fries. That's when I discovered that he could cook his own fries in the deep fryer. I did not realize how closely he had been watching me, because cooking was not something I would have taught him. He also likes to empty the whole bottle of cooking oil, so I hide that too.

We went through a phase when he would break glass. He accidentally knocked a picture off the wall and the glass broke. Then he started taking pictures off the wall and breaking the glass on purpose. There would be a pile of glass on the floor and I would rush to clean it up because I was afraid he would cut himself. One day, I was angry enough just to leave the broken glass on the floor. He was very careful not to cut himself. I made him sweep it up himself. Of course, I went behind him to make sure that there really was no more glass on the floor. He was angry because he does not like to be told what to do, but he stopped breaking glass.

During the "breaking glass" phase (though he has been toilet trained for years), he was also urinating and defecating on the floor in the living room. Of all places, the living room! This was not by accident because he would pull his pants down so as not to soil them. This was during the time I was teaching, and upon coming home I would walk in the door to the sights and smells of these gifts he was leaving me. I truly could not stand this! Talk about bizarre! This only stopped once I started leaving it on the floor for a while. This was hard! Then I would make him clean it up. (Of course, that made more of a mess for me to clean up for real). These were two of his actions that made me decide again that I would have to find a place to put him if he did not stop.

The problem was that one of his medications had been discontinued by the pharmaceutical company and we would have to find another medication to replace it. We finally found the right combination of medications.

I can't stand it when he yelps and yells. He is so loud! He makes these noises when we are watching TV, which usually causes me to miss something I really wanted to hear. Or he will make these noises when we are in public and all eyes will be on us again – "The Claudreen and PJ sideshow."

I can't stand the fact that I can never leave home without making arrangements for PJ. If I am going on a trip, it has to be well planned. I can't do any spur of the moment activities.

As long as I have PJ at home, I will always need help.

I see myself as someone who does the helping, not as the one that has to be helped. That was hard for me to accept. I am thankful that I have such a great support system in my children and my parents who don't mind helping.

I cannot stand it when he masturbates, though he has learned to be discreet about it and go to his room. His teacher at Burger managed to get that across to him by showing him pictures of his bedroom with the door open and with the door closed.

There is something that I do that PJ cannot stand. He does not like to hear me laugh. (My daughter Stephanie says that's because my laugh is a cackle). I have learned to laugh silently. There were years that I did not laugh at all, because I was so depressed. It's now important to me to have a reason to laugh because laughter is healthy. (Situation comedies help me with this.)

When he is doing something that I cannot stand, I talk to God about this situation. I have not always been respectful, but God has forgiven me because He understands.

Chapter Seven

He Ain't Heavy, He's My Son

*The road is long with many a winding turn
That leads us to who knows where,
who knows when
But I am strong,
I'm strong enough to carry him
He ain't heavy, he's my son.*

I REMEMBER WHEN PJ was extremely heavy, when I was burdened down by the full weight of his autism. But now I am looking at autism from the other end of the autism spectrum – the vantage point of age and experience, having survived it.

I see that a lot of the things that I was afraid would happen did not happen and a lot of the things that I hoped would happen also did not happen. PJ and I have both grown. I thought that I was "grown" when he came along, but I had no idea how much growing I was going to have to do.

That growth has been one of the blessings of my struggles with him. I am bigger, better, stronger and healthier than I was when he was born. I have plans for brighter days ahead At the age of sixty-eight, I am looking forward to a grand future. I have a couple of projects that I want to complete, and I have Faith that I will live long enough to complete them. I've asked God for sufficient days to reach my goals because I lost a lot of time being overwhelmed by autism.

I'd thought that my son's autism was going to ruin my life, and for a while I believed this. His autism had a great impact on my life, but it did not ruin it. My faith in God has been confirmed and strengthened. I learned that faith has to come before the results. If you already know the outcome, then you don't need faith. I could not have lived with PJ for 32 years ??? without faith. I could not make plans for the future without faith. I would rather keep the faith for years and then be disappointed, than be disappointed for years because I had no faith.

I worried about his future until I decided that I would be his future. I decided that I would be his future because any other option was too painful for me. I have never regretted that decision (well, almost never). I worried about us missing the "window of opportunity" to cure him. I realize that all persons with autism can't be "cured," and PJ was one of those persons. But does that mean that he has less worth as a person? Not to me. It means that he is a unique person but he is still a person, worthy of my love and my time. This is something I had to learn from other parents and teachers of children with disabilities.

I have quit apologizing for him. I gave PJ birth, but God gave him life, so he is entitled to his little space on this planet just like the rest of us. He, too, is a child of God, cured or not cured. In his book, "The Prophet," Kahlil Gibran writes, "Your children are not your children. They are the sons and daughters of life's longing for itself. They come through you, but not from you." Reading this passage always gave me great comfort.

Thank God that people with disabilities have "rights." If PJ had come along 10 years sooner he would not have had these rights. He has the right to life. He has the right to an education up to whatever his level his ability will allow. He will never be a doctor or lawyer or make an important contribution to society (I've had this fact pointed out to me). But he could be and is a better person because of special education and the special education mission that no matter what the disability, the person is entitled to a "free and appropriate education in the least restrictive environment."

Thank God that he came along after these laws were passed. Isn't one of the measures of a society how it treats the poor, the disabled and the elderly? If he had been born even a year earlier, our lives might have been totally different because I did not know any better.

He has the right to liberty and the pursuit of happiness, however, he perceives it. He has the right not to be abused. He has the right to health and contentment. He has the right to live in the community as long as we make sure that his rights to not interfere with the rights of others to have peace and not be disturbed.

I've learned a lot from PJ. I've learned about unconditional love. He loves me no matter what. No matter what I am wearing; whether my hair is combed or my teeth are brushed; whether I am going to buy him something or take him somewhere; or whether I have any money, PJ Jr. gives me such a look of love, that if it were coming from someone else, I would wonder what they wanted from me. It is a look that I never thought I would get from him during the days when I wondered if he would ever love me back, or if I would continue to love him if he were not brought out of his autism. It is a look of pure love that radiates from him. I have learned to love him unconditionally: he can't help that he has autism. When a person has a disability, should we be angry with him and blame him for a situation that is beyond his control?

PJ has taught me to live in the present. He does not worry about the future or the past. Living in the present is very difficult for me, especially being his mother, but it is one of the reasons I have survived thus far. Reading the book, "I'm Not Much, But I'm All I've Got" taught me that sometimes you have to take life five minutes at a time. You have to tell yourself that there is nothing that will happen to me in the next five minutes that I can't handle.

I've learned from him how to tune out things that are worthy of being tuned out. Some things are not worth my full time and attention. Although PJ tunes too many things out, it is one of his survival strategies. It has become one of mine, too.

He is thirty-two years old, and has a good "quality of life," which is all I had the power to give him. He loves listening to music, skating and bowling. He loves cooking his own fries and sausage. He loves to hang out in the kitchen and watch me cook (which is seldom). He loves helping cook some dishes, such as spaghetti and cornbread, though he may not eat them. He loves running the washer and dishwasher, though he doesn't care whether or not they are empty.

He was the catalyst for PJ Sr. and me getting back together. After being separated for more than a dozen years, we came together again. We both had PJ's best interests in mind all during our separation. PJ was our common ground. I never thought that we would get back together, but that is proof that God is still working miracles in the world.

I had to forgive PJ Sr. I'd read that forgiveness is more important for the person doing the forgiving than for the one who has to be forgiven. It's true. Once I forgave, a load was lifted and I actually felt lighter.

We were never divorced. I had filed for divorce when I first left him and we had both hired lawyers. My lawyer became a judge and PJ Sr.'s lawyer's office was firebombed by a disgruntled client. Neither one of us ever chose a different lawyer after that. I always thought I would eventually get another lawyer, but I never did, so we stayed married.

"What God has joined together" took a lot of twists and turns in our marriage and had a completely different outcome than I expected. Yet, PJ Sr. always said we would get back together, which is why he did not get another lawyer. I always thought, "How wrong can he be?"

One of PJ Sr.'s hit records was "Working My Way Back to You, Babe." He said he always felt we were working our way back to each other; I always felt that we had come to the end of our road together. Once again, he gave me a lesson in perseverance and faith.

He has always been a great father to PJ and showed appreciation for my efforts to mother this difficult child. He was always there when I needed help with PJ; all I had to do was call. He would take PJ out with him at times and felt that people should accept his son, even when his son was unacceptable. I had to admire the father that he was even when I did not like him.

We have all been accepting of PJ, but sometimes I wonder if we accepted the son that God gave us or the son that became handicapped by the vaccine.

Though I believe that the vaccine given to him in 1976 is partially responsible for his condition, I would never advocate discontinuing vaccines. They are extremely important and if we discontinued them, we would have an even worse situation on our hands. I don't know what the solution is in this case. Maybe the vaccine triggers something in some babies that is already there. My older children all had their vaccines and it did not hurt them.

I was discussing the vaccine dilemma with a doctor during one of my committee meetings. His theory was that even if it was discovered that the vaccine caused autism in 5% of the population that still meant that the majority of people benefited so vaccines would continue. I agreed with him, but that 5% number has grown since then.

I've lived with autism for 32 years and still have no answers. The only treatments that have helped people with autism are extremely time consuming and expensive, so they are not available to everyone. According to the Autism Society of America, national statistics show that the number of Americans with autism spectrum disorder is still growing. I am shocked and saddened that so many more children are being diagnosed with the condition. My thoughts and prayers are with them and their parents. I thought that by the time PJ was an adult we would have more answers and less people with autism.

From my observations of my son, I do think that there is faulty wiring in the brain, (a neurological disorder). There is not a blueprint for this faulty wiring and it is different in different people, so some can be reversed and some cannot.

When he was fifteen, he started having seizures, and is still taking medication for control of his seizures. At one point, we decided to see if he still needed seizure medication. We stopped giving him the medicine and everything seemed to be all right, until we went on a trip with his father.

The group was appearing on Mackinac Island, one of my favorite places in Michigan. There are no cars on this historic island. You get around by horse drawn carriage or bicycle. The morning that we were leaving to come back home, PJ collapsed as he was coming out of the bathroom. I felt terrible because that could have been avoided if he'd taken his medication. We had to walk to the ferry location to take a ferry to where cars and buses were parked. Then we had a four hour bus ride back to Detroit. PJ was tired and lethargic after a seizure, and I was still feeling terrible. What a time for him to have a seizure!

I never stopped his seizure medication again. The doctor said that the only way to tell if he is now seizure free is to stop giving him the medication. Since he has already had a seizure in the worst possible place at the worse possible time, I am not willing to take that chance. I don't know if seizures are a part of his neurological disorder or not.

I also believe that there is a hormonal imbalance that gets out of control at times. I believe that a release of certain hormones trigger aggression or fear, both of which cause aggressive or hostile behavior in PJ. I think that there are also feel good hormones that sometimes get triggered.

He has laughing spells and has a hard time controlling his positive feelings, like excitement as well as his negative feelings, like anger and rage. He has poor impulse control and does not have the ability to achieve higher levels of thinking. He can not get past a certain point in his thinking and is not aware of his affect on other people.

Since Michigan is a state where people with severe disabilities can attend school (thank God) until age 26, I'd hoped that somewhere along the way, there would be an answer.

He has always been in schools and programs specifically for people with autism, which are considered as segregated facilities. Many parents of autistic children feel that being "mainstreamed" is the best solution for them, and I agree with their choice because their children are higher on the autism spectrum and have more ability than PJ. I still feel that PJ's teachers have always done their best with him and I was not comfortable with mainstreaming.

Though he was never mainstreamed in school, he is with normal people after school and in the community. I don't believe mainstreaming would have worked with him, but if you're a reader who has experienced mainstreaming, I welcome your feedback.

PJ will not be able to live or work independently, but he is not aware enough to care so it is not a problem to him. He will always have to live in a structured environment with caregivers. I am not worried about him being restrained or abused any more because society has come a long way with the treatment of people like PJ. He is no longer abusive to himself or other people. As long as he takes his medication, he is pleasant and agreeable.

He tries to follow instructions and to cooperate. He has much greater self-control and realizes that pushing or hitting people hurts them, and he doesn't want to hurt anyone.

He is basically a happy young man. No one is 100% happy, so I think he is about as happy as the rest of us; maybe more. He's not worried about bills, terrorism, love life, etc. I said that I would have to adjust to him because he couldn't adjust to me, but he did make an adjustment or I would not have been able to live with him all the time. I may have missed some windows of opportunity, but I've had teachable moments with him. For instance, I would go on strike if he behaved in a manner that was abusive to me. I would sit down and refuse to move until his behavior improved.

I don't know if he will ever realize how different he is, but if he does realize it, he can say, "They loved me anyhow."

He has inspired and motivated me (as you can see). Our story is not a sad story, though it is not the story I would have wanted to write. I would have wanted to write about him coming out of autism and living and working independently. I would have wanted to write about the treatments we used to accomplish this. I would have wanted to write that research had discovered the cause of autism.

Because he cannot speak, I found my voice to speak for him and others like him. I am thankful that I live in America where I have the right to free speech. I did not realize how important free speech is until I started meeting people who could not speak.

8

Chapter Eight

How I got Oo-ver, How I got Oo-ver
My soul looks back and wonders
How I got over.

I KNOW HOW I got over. It takes a village to raise a child or raise a woman from her bed of depression and help her get back on her feet and moving forward again. These people are my Village – my heroes who helped restore my soul.

I've had parents of newly identified children with autism tell me that I was a hero. I accept! We need more heroes. But I can only accept that label if we recognize that every parent who is struggling with a child with a disability, or every person with a disability who is struggling to live a normal life is a hero. Able bodied and able minded people have no idea how hard their lives are.

If you have a friend or a relative with a disabled child, think about being a voluntary hero for them. Could you offer to sit with their child for a day or night to give them a little respite and freedom for a few hours? If you can not bring yourself to do this, then you realize just how much of a hero they are. Could you volunteer to help with housecleaning for a few hours a week? Could you fix (or buy) dinner for them every once in a while, so they don't have to cook that day. Can you say to them; "I'm sorry for what you're going through. What can I do to help?" Like I said, "We need more Heroes".

My older children were my first heroes because whenever I needed a break from PJ, they were there and available to keep him while I made my escape to normalcy for a few hours. I really don't know what I would have done without them being there to give me a few moments of peace. They have always had my back.

They also lifted my spirits when I was down. I'd say, "At least I have three normal children."

My three "normal" children would all hold up two fingers.

"Are you saying I have only two normal children?" I'd ask.

They'd all nod "yes."

"Well, who else is not a normal child?"

They would all point to each other.

This always made me laugh.

I've already told you about my oldest daughter Cindy, who assigned me "required reading" that helped me realize that I was not alone in my "Twilight Zone" life. The books she provided or recommended showed me that other parents had survived their difficult children.

My parents, Herbert and Grace Gilbert, also have become my heroes. They stay with PJ sometimes so that I can go on a trip or an outing when I need a little rest and relaxation. Now that his behavior has improved, I don't worry about leaving him with them. PJ loves them and does not give them any trouble. He cooks his own French fries and sausage and is very independent as long as they don't give him too many instructions.

His sister, Stephanie, helps me with him a great deal. She takes him home with her and keeps him at least one weekend a month. She also takes him on outings. She spends so much time with him that PJ probably thinks that she is his assistant mother. Thanks to Stephanie and my parents, I have more freedom of movement.

Parents of children with disabilities are my heroes. It was from them that I learned that parenting an autistic child was not impossible. It could be done. These parents had pushed for special education for handicapped children. I was in school in the 40s and 50s before special education programs were established. The more severely impaired children were kept at home, the less severely impaired just sat in the back of the room and were ignored by everyone. Not as bad as throwing rocks at them in the schoolyard, but not an education.

I am thankful for special education, but we seem to be losing some of the gains that we made. Dr. Draper used to say: "There is something "special" about special education." She was right. It is my hope that the mainstreaming movement does not send us backward and cause us to forget that some students will always need small classrooms and teachers' aides. I think we will always need some disability-specific classrooms. I don't see it as segregated; I see it as giving the child what is appropriate for his or her condition.

Teachers are my heroes, especially special education teachers. Special education teachers have a higher tolerance for deviant behavior. We used to say that regular education teachers teach material and special education teachers teach children. Regular education teachers have so much stress and pressure to have children do well on standardized tests that sometimes they can't focus on what the children really need to learn.

Special education teachers have more flexibility to re-teach and tailor the lesson to the individual child. A special education teacher in Detroit taught me strategies to use to control PJ's, extremely defiant behavior. I could not believe that she was willing to take him on. Not only did she take him on, she taught him to be civilized, not to mention toilet training him.

The special education teachers at Burger always gave me their home phone numbers and welcomed me to call them if necessary. I appreciated this so much that when I became a teacher, I gave the parents of my students my home phone number. If they ever had a question, they could call me. They never abused the privilege, nor did I.

It was also the teachers at Burger who arranged for me to produce and host a cable television show about autism in 1988 and 1989. I was in college and about to get my Bachelor's degree, so I could not focus on the show as much as I would have liked. I called the show "My Piece of the Puzzle" because the symbol for autism is a puzzle. I had no answers – all I had was a piece of the puzzle.

I so appreciated special education teachers that I was motivated to go back to school to become one. I wanted to do for another parent what had been done for me. I wanted to join Dr. Draper in her efforts to educate children with handicaps. Special education was at its best when she was the director, because she fought for advances for the students and listened to parents' concerns.

When I was teaching, my principal, Johnnie Gilmore, became one of my heroes. It took a great deal of effort to try to be a good teacher at my age, as well as a mother to PJ. I tried to do extra because since I started so late, I wanted to make up for lost time. On a number of occasions, my energy was low due to my trials with PJ or challenges with my students. She recognized the extra effort that I put forth and recommended me for various awards. I don't know if she ever knew how much this meant to me. This recognition from her fueled me to continue to do my best and to go on at times when I felt I had nothing left to give.

I've already told you about Bill Walsh who was director of the Michigan Society for Autistic Citizens (MSAC), which is now Autism Society of Michigan (ASM). When I became a member of the board of directors, he had faith in me when I did not have faith in myself. He put me to work as an advocate for people with autism. It was something that I wanted done bad enough to do it myself. If not me, then who? Who else cared enough to put themselves out there without a net? I needed encouragement and support and he provided that. He arranged for PJ and me to be filmed as a part of a documentary about autism. The show was called "Survival." I did not know then whether or not I was going to survive.

Governors Jim Blanchard and John Engler were my heroes because they were concerned enough about people with disabilities in the state of Michigan to have advisory committees to let them know what was needed. We would meet with one another and make recommendations to the governors. When Blanchard was governor, Michigan had a national reputation for exemplary programs for people with disabilities.

Gov. Blanchard used to have Sunday brunches for all his advisory committee members. He had over 100 advisory committees concerning various aspects of situations in the state. He invited us to the Governor's summer home on Mackinac Island, one of the most beautiful locations in the state, a place where three of the Great Lakes come together. We were able to spend the afternoon in that beautiful location, visiting with the Governor. This is one of my favorite memories. It was a special treat because after a four-hour drive, we spent the night at a hotel before going to the governor's mansion for brunch.

Eunice Kennedy Shriver is one of my heroes, because she started the Special Olympics. There were no athletic programs for children with disabilities before then. PJ is so active and athletic that he needed an outlet for his energy. Once again, he could not be mainstreamed. Even though he had talent, he could not understand all the rules and regulations to play on any kind of team.

Dustin Hoffman and Tom Cruise, in the movie "Rainman," became my heroes, along with the writer, Ronald Bass who won an Academy Award for best screenplay. It was quite accurate.

Anyone who has dealt with autism could tell that a lot of time and effort was invested in making the movie as credible as possible. Dustin played the part with great believability. I saw a TV show about the autistic man that the story Rainman was based on. He is now in his fifties and is still being taken care of by his father who is in his eighties. Talk about a hero!

Other movies about autism have impressed me as well. "Family Pictures," starring Angelica Houston was a convincing portrayal of problems that the families face. "Miracle Run," a movie about a single mother of twins who had autism, also did a good job of portraying the plight of autistic children and their parents.

I don't know who wrote it, but I love this quote "From the bottom of the deepest pit, if you look up, you can still see the stars." And to my heroes whose books helped me to look up, to get up, to stay up and to start moving, I'd like to quote PJ Sr., "Sometimes God wants you to get up off your knees and go do something." My heroes helped me with this. I still read something inspirational every day from one of these books.

Some of my heroes came along before PJ. When I was fourteen years old and was grappling with a certain problem, I remember sitting in church while the choir was singing, "He Knows Just How Much We Can Bear." "Is that true? Lord, I've had all I can bear. Please help me." A weight was lifted from my young shoulders, and I realized that God is really there.

Many years later, when I was a physical and emotional wreck from dealing with PJ, I read "Yoga, Youth and Reincarnation" by Jess Stearn. That book sent me to a yoga class that helped me physically, emotionally and spiritually.

Although I'd stopped for a few years, I am doing yoga again and can notice a difference in how I look and feel.

Dr. Norman Vincent Peale wrote about "The Power of Positive Thinking." He taught me that I could change my life simply by changing my attitude. He said that "the facts are not as important as your attitude about the facts." You can't change what happens to you, but you can change how you feel about what happens to you. In his booklet, "Thought Conditioners," he gives specific tips for changing your attitude. I knew that PJ could not change his attitude, so I had to change mine. He still has autism, but "Thought Conditioners" helped me to change my attitude about it. The attitude is more important than the facts.

Dr. Peale also said that "God created us and He can constantly and automatically recreate us." I am so thankful that I discovered the power of Dr. Peale's teachings. When I was at my lowest point, I would read his words over and over until they "took."

In "Your Erroneous Zones," Dr. Wayne Dyer also helped me. He said that you can control your feelings because you can change your thoughts about your feelings. You can take charge of yourself through your thoughts and actions. He also reminds us to consider the consequences before we make a decision.

In "The Renewing Power of Your Mind," I read that the mind was created with the capacity to constantly renew itself. I read this book at a time that my mind was foggy and clouded by my total focus on autism and I did not know if it was true or not. It is true.

*Be ye transformed by the renewing of your mind.
(Romans 12:2)*

He restores my soul. (Psalms 23:3)

So many writers with the same message on how we can renew ourselves.

Dr. Loma Wing, in her book, "Autistic Children" helped me to understand PJ's behavior. As did Temple Grandin in her book "Emergence, Labeled Autism." They helped me to see things from PJ's perspective, instead of wallowing in my own. I realized that his feelings were beyond his control at times. I really respect and admire Temple for all she did to overcome her autism and for giving us insight into her thoughts.

Some of our gospel music gave me great comfort. PJ likes music, too, so sometimes it calmed him. At a financial and emotional low point in my life, we listened to Al Green's recording of "The Lord Will Make a Way, Somehow" everyday. Each time I heard it, I felt better and better and the Lord did make a way.

In her book "Return to Love," among other things Marianne Williamson taught me to forgive those who had hurt me. I forgave my husband. We forgave each other, decided to leave the past in the past and ended up getting back together. God is still working Miracles in this world! In the words of another one of his songs, "A tiny spark will remain, and sparks turn into flame, and love can burn once again. (I'll Be Around)

In "The Greatest Miracle in The World," Og Mandino tells us that we are capable of so much more than we give ourselves credit for. If you are at a low point in your life, this book gives you a lot to think about and a lot of hope. This book was one of the motivations for me to go back to college, get two degrees and become a special education teacher.

In "The Greatest Salesman in the World," Mr. Mandino presents the tools that can lead to a better life. Among other things, he teaches how to "master your emotions" and to "greet the world with love in your heart."

Agnes Sanford, in "Healing Gifts of the Spirit" reminds us that inside of us, is a little pilot light that never goes out. That no matter how bad or hopeless we feel, our pilot light is still burning. (The spark that can turn into a flame).

In her book, "In the Spirit," Susan Taylor reminds us that "What we send out into the Universe is what we get back). She also says that the more unlovable a person appears, the more in need of love he or she is." This helped me with my students as well as with PJ. She also reminds us that God created us to be creators ourselves.

"Simple Abundance," by Sarah Ban Breathnach is another book that I have read more than once. She is teaching me how to uncover the "authentic me." (A "me" that had gotten lost in autism). She teaches us how to incorporate gratitude, simplicity, order, harmony, beauty and joy in our daily life. (I am working on these principles and will probably never get it all together). That's OK, because she helps us accept the person we are as we move toward the person we want to be.

Oprah Winfrey has taught me that if you work hard and listen to the Spirit within, your accomplishments can grow, whatever your race, gender or weight. What a wonderful teacher she is! I can't accomplish what she has, but I can accomplish more than I have and I intend to. She is proof that you cannot help anyone else without helping yourself.

Montel Williams has taught me that we have the power within to overcome anything. After his successes and accomplishments, he was hit with a condition that has devastated others, but he did not let it stop him. I know what amazing courage and fortitude he must have to not miss a beat in his life. In the book "Climbing Higher," he tells us of his ups and downs.

Les Brown told us "Don't die with your music still in you." In studies of people on their deathbed their biggest regrets were not about things that they did, but about things that they wanted to do, but didn't. That is why I decided to write this book at my advanced age. I can try to help my heroes to spread a positive message.

The movie "Son Rise" was the first one I ever saw about autism more than twenty years ago. This movie showed just how much parents go through in order to "cure" their child with autism.

Autism is such a baffling disorder that I am impressed when the writers and actors get it right, as they did in two documentaries that I saw in April 2008. April is National Autism Month and in April 2008, the media presented shows to promote autism awareness and understanding. I did not see everything, but of what I saw, two documentaries really impressed me.

"Autism: Oh the Possibilities," is full of good information about autism and about the professionals who work with people with the condition. They discussed ABA (Applied Behavior Analysis), which is a behavioral intervention program to help with behavior problems. (It is too expensive for many of us, but greatly helpful to those who can afford it). The show addressed the mercury in the vaccine situation by explaining that some children excrete mercury and some don't. There are things that can interfere with the excretion of mercury.

The program gives tips on the diagnosis of autism, such as making note of their development; of their individual cognitive processing difficulties (do they understand what is done or said?); and of their relationship to others. It gives tips on how to relate to people with autism, such as following the lead of that person, seeing what they are interested in and building on their interests. The documentary has so much more information than I can relate here that it is well worth watching.

The other program that really impressed me was "Autism, The Musical" It focused on the Miracle Project run by Elaine Hill who led autistic children in writing, rehearsing and performing a musical. I don't know how she had the courage to even attempt such a daunting project. The show included interviews with autistic children and their parents both of whom shared their perspectives. In addition, "Autism, The Musical," explored the struggles parents and children had to endure while trying to create a musical and make it a success.

Of course, I have many heroes from the Bible, but I will mention again Isaiah 40:31: *"They that wait on the Lord will renew their strength..."*

As I look back from this end of the autism spectrum, I can see how God sent me just what I needed when the time was right. Have you heard the song "He may not come when you call Him, but He's right on time"?

Each one of my heroes helped me in some way. They turned on lights for me when I was in the dark. They gave me energy when my own energy was gone. They gave me a reason to have Faith when all my hope was gone. They gave me comfort when I needed comfort. They proved to me that our bodies and minds can be renewed and restored.

Glory, Glory, Hallelujah! Since I laid by burdens down!

Chapter Nine

To Everything There Is A Season

To every thing there is a season and a time to every purpose under the heaven. A time to be born and a time to die; a time to break down and a time to build up; a time to weep and a time to laugh: a time to mourn and a time to dance (Ecclesiastes 3:1-4).

THIS IS THE chapter that I neither wanted nor expected to write, because it is about the death of my husband, PJ, Sr. So came my time to weep and my time to mourn. My time to mourn came as a shock because it happened so fast.

PJ, Sr. performed what turned out to be his last engagement on July 19th, 2008 in California. He told me that he could not make it to the next engagement on July 29th, because he was not feeling well. I was concerned because he never missed an engagement, but I was not yet alarmed. We made two visits to the doctor, he was hospitalized twice and by August 18th, he was gone. A CAT scan the week before his death showed a number of tumors, but I did not get a diagnosis of cancer until two days before he died.

We all knew that he was going downhill fast, but he always lived his life fast, so I kept expecting a turn for the better. We kept a close watch on him. Someone was in the hospital room with him at all times. Our oldest daughter, Cindy was spending nights there on a cot in his room. It was she who called me about 1:30 a.m. to tell me that he wasn't breathing.

The other children and I rushed to the hospital and spent two and a half hours in this room, crying and praying. But he wasn't waking up. He had slipped quietly and peacefully away. My head knew this, my heart did not believe what had happened.

Once the news of his death circulated, the house began to fill with people. People were bringing food, drinks, flowers and sympathy. Friends and relatives took over the daily chores and answered phone calls, because I had a funeral to plan.

In the midst of the crowds and confusion, I was still sending PJ to his day program at Damon's House because I wanted his life to remain as normal as possible. I was concerned, though, about how he would react to all the people when he came home each day. I was hoping that he did not lose the self-control gains he had made.

He reacted in a not so surprising way. He retreated, just like his father used to do, by hiding out in our bedroom. He even took over his father's side of the bed. It was his regular routine when PJ, Sr. was out of town; so now it was his retreat. He would come home, get something to eat and head upstairs to the bedroom. We would turn the TV to one of the Music Choice channels, he would close the door to shut out all the noises from downstairs and spend the evening there.

During such a busy, hectic, crowd-filled week PJ was no trouble at all. When my husband's body was ready for a private viewing, we took PJ for his last look at his father, not knowing how he would react. I waited and watched. After sitting and staring for a while, he moved across the room, stood by the casket and laid his head on his father's chest and remained there about three minutes. He rubbed his father's hair, touched his face tenderly, and then stared at his face for a few minutes, as if to see if he would open his eyes. It was an extremely touching sight.

When I was telling a friend about PJ's reaction, I mentioned that I did not know how much he understood of what had happened. He said that PJ knew something was different because, PJ, Sr. did not reach out to him as he usually did.

We did not take PJ to the family hour or the funeral. The night of the funeral, there were a lot of people at the house. I'd mentioned to one of the members of my husband's group that PJ could sing. He asked PJ to sing. Our daughter, Stephanie, who also sings, started singing PJ's favorite songs. PJ sang with her. He laughed; he danced; he sang; he clapped his hands in tandem with the applause of our family and friends who were watching. He was performing for the people instead of retreating, much like his father, who never missed a chance to perform. He was having fun! It was a surprising ending to such a sad day.

So, once again, we faced an uncertain future, but my faith was still strong, because I know that "He who holds the future, also holds my hands."

10
Chapter Ten

Poetry Inspired By Autism

riting poetry was my therapy. Writing my feelings down whether they rhymed or made sense to anyone other than me didn't matter. It gave me a sense of control and accomplishment. Sometimes my world felt like it was spinning out of control and writing poetry gave me just enough of a sense of control that I felt like I could keep going. Even on my worst days, if I could put something down on paper it would make that day a little better.

My goal in sharing my poetry with you is to let you know that you are not alone. I want you to know there are other people out there who really understand your ups, your downs, your smiles and your frowns. And no matter how bad you are feeling right now there are brighter days ahead. I am the proof in the pudding.

LITTLE LOST CHILD

This is how I felt when I first found out about PJ's autism.

Your little lost child
Is looking for you.
Don't know where to go,
Don't know what to do.

My light's going out
And it's getting cold.
And I feel so tired,
And I feel so old.

Don't know how I'll make it
To get through the day
Without help from you
To show me the way.

Your little lost child,
I'm down on my knees.
Can't get up by myself,
So, Lord, help me please.

If you take my hand,
I'll make one more mile.
So reach down and touch
Your little lost child.

He did!

I sought the Lord, and He heard me, and delivered me from all my fears (Psalm 34:4).

MY OLD MAN

When PJ was younger, he was frustrated, hostile and aggressive, as are many children who are handicapped by autism. Many times, I was in tears, but sometimes I could see the humor in the situation. My Old Man and Dr. Jekyll were written about PJ in one of my rare moments of humor. As he got older, I've had more moments of humor about him.

He yelled at me this morning
When his breakfast egg was late,
And when I put his bacon on,
He pushed away his plate.

I thought that I could deal with him
by giving him a kiss,
But he snarled at me and turned his head
And pushed me with his fist.

I said, Oh well. He'll brighten up.
I'll fix his favorite drink.
He took the glass and frowned at me
And threw it in the sink.

So then I got his pants unzipped,
And tried to pull them down.
He snatched from me,
And ran away and made an angry sound.

I thought I'd try to talk to him,
Cause I was getting mad.
But he wouldn't listen to me,
Which made me feel real bad.

So I took him in the bedroom
And put him in the bed.
It's the only thing that works, I thought,
I kissed his smooth forehead.

I tucked the covers round him,
Don't want him catching cold.
Cause he's a mess when he is sick,
And he's only two years old.

Claudreen Jackson

DR. JEKYLL AND MR. HYDE

He was sittin' and smilin'
And his eyes were bright.
He looked so sweet and innocent
Like he would never fight.
So, I thought I'd get a little kiss
While he was in the mood.
What made me think that he'd be good
When he was always rude?
I got no kiss, I got a slap.
I don't know why I tried.
Cause he's a Dr. Jekyll and a Mr. Hyde

He fell down and hurt himself
And I was holding out my arms,
Cause he was still my baby
And I didn't want him harmed.
I picked him up and kissed him,
And he hit me on the head.
I'd thought that I could pet him,
But I got hurt, instead.
Why'd I think I could console
By rushing to his side?
When he's a Dr. Jekyll and a Mr. Hyde.

He woke up and came to me
And climbed into my lap.
So, I got ready for a hug,
But what I got was slapped.

I put him down and walked away.
And he stood there and cried.
He really has a lot of nerve.
That little Mr. Hyde.

He was reaching out to touch me,
But I had backed away.
I wasn't taking any chances.
Cause I'd been hurt today
By his pinchin' and his scratchin'
And I was tired and sick
Of this little kid they said was mine.
I'd get away, right quick.
But he was reaching out his arms again,
And I could not resist.
So, I picked him up and held him close,
And he gave me a kiss
And put his arms around me.
My heart just swelled with pride.
I love my Dr. Jekyll
And my little Mr. Hyde.

SPECIAL SPECIAL EDUCATOR

I can't say enough about the teachers and therapists who work with children with autism. They were the ones who helped me learn to accept my son and learn to manage(?) his behavior. They are truly earning their stars in Heaven. I wish I could give them all medals.

Special is as special does,
And special you shall be
when you care for special people
Who are not like you and me.

You're trying to "save the children,"
And you're doing it with grace
And love and dedication,
And a smile upon your face.

You all are special people.
You taught me how to see,
To look into the inside, and let the outside be.

Your determination caught me.
I can make it if I try.
I'm learning to be patient,
I'm learning not to cry.

I'm learning to be positive.
I'll do what I can do.
And if I make some progress
It's what I've learned from you.

I don't know why you do it.
I don't know why you care.
But I have to tell you how I feel.
Thank God that you are there.

Claudreen Jackson

HEAVEN'S VERY SPECIAL CHILD

I don't know if this poem was inspired by autism because I did not write it. The writer is anonymous. I included it because it gave me a great deal of comfort when I needed to be comforted. It was given to me by one of PJ's teachers.

A meeting was held far from Earth.
It's time again for another birth,
Said the angels to the Lord above,
This special child will need much love.

His progress may seem very slow,
Accomplishments, he may not show.
And he'll require some extra care
From the folks he meets down there.

He may not run, laugh or play.
His thoughts may seem quite far away.
In many ways, he won't adapt,
And some may say he's handicapped.

So, let's be careful where he's sent.
We want his life to be content.
Please, Lord, find the parents who
Will do a special job for you.

They may not realize right away
The leading role they're asked to play,
But with this child sent from above,
Comes stronger faith and richer love.

And soon, they'll know the privilege given
In caring for this gift from Heaven.
Their precious charge, so meek and mild
Is Heaven's very special child.

Anonymous

SPECIAL SPECIAL PARENT

When I was trying to decide how to mother this difficult child, I joined several parenting organizations. We all had children who were handicapped, though not all were autistic. These parents were so dedicated and committed to making life better for their children that I learned from them. A parent struggling with a handicapped child is a true unsung hero.

Most special of the special ones,
You were my Guiding Light.
When it was cold and it was dark,
And life was black as night.

When I was cold and I was scared,
And lived in lonely fear.
You showed me just what I could do,
And helped me dry my tears.

Though you could not cure my son,
You helped me to cure me.
You turned on lights to chase the dark
So I could plainly see.

Now, I know that you get weary,
And I know that you get worn,
But you have earned your star in Heaven
Since the day your child was born.

I know you've had some sleepless nights,
And you could use some rest.
But love is shining through the worn spots.
I believe you're truly blessed.

Though I'd like to give you medals
To show you that I care,
All I can do is give you love
And remember you in prayer.

Claudreen Jackson

IF I ONLY HAD A DAY

I did finally manage to get that day. Down through the years I have managed to do all the things that I mention in the poem.

If I only had a day
To wash my cares away,
To soak in the tub, to get a back rub.
To find the me that I used to be.
Do I still have an identity?

If I had a day without this child
Would I feel that I could smile?
Maybe for a little while
I could go to visit friends
And reacquaint myself with them.
And I could feel like me again.

Could I go to see a show?
Relax and laugh and let troubles go?
Could I go to dinner and see how it feels
To eat a good meal that is real?

If I only had a day
Would I find a way
To catch up on my chores,
To sweep all my floors?
To make my house all nice and clean
So I could have some company?

If I only had a day
Would I have a chance to say
All the things that are on my mind,
To feel like I have free time
To try on my clothes,
To polish my toes.
To exhale at last
To complete a big task.

I'm tired of cryin'
I want to start tryin'
To put things back together again.
But I need a day
To find my way
It's coming, but I don't know when.

This mothering that never ends
I'm smothering in all the trends
I really try to do my best,
But don't know if I pass the test
In trying to manage all my stress.
So if I only had a day
Could I find the proper way?

Some time to work
Some time to play?
Or would I just go
To bed and stay?

THERE'S SOMETHING GOING ON
THAT I'M MISSING

My son still can not talk, but I have talked to high functioning people with autism that can. I talk to them every chance I get in order to get some insight. I think this is sometimes how they feel. This is also sometimes how I feel.

As I watched a TV show,
I said, "There's one thing that I know,
There's something going on that I'm missing."
I can figure out the plot,
but there's something I cannot
There's something going on that I'm missing.

Well, I went to a ballet,
and watched the dancer's pirouette,
But there was something going on that I was missing.
I could see them spin and glide
Cause my eyes were open wide,
But there was something going on that I was missing.

As I watched a football game,
Thinking every games the same,
There was something going on that I was missing
The player picked up his bat,
And I was real sure that
There was something going on that I was missing.

I don't know what life is about,
Going in and coming out.
There is something going on that I'm missing.
So, When it comes my final day,
I might not even know, I'll say,
There is something going on that I'm missing.

SPECIAL SPECIAL KID

With thanks to Rogers and Hart.

You are my little special child
My funny valentine.
An accident of Providence?
Or are you by design?

It matters not the answer,
for you are here with me.
That you're not like the other kids
Is mighty plain to see.

But you are a worthy person
Who has come a long, long way.
Helping you has helped me grow
To where I am today.

There's something I must tell you,
Though the words are nothing new.
They've been sung so many times.
I say them now to you.

Is your figure less than Greek?
Is your mouth a little weak?
When you open it to speak
Are you smart?

Though other folks may think you odd,
You're my favorite work of art.
My funny little valentine,
You've slipped into my heart.

Claudreen Jackson

WILL THERE BE A HAPPY ENDING?

Faith is when you believe that your situation will turn out all right even when the cause seems hopeless. I would rather keep the Faith for years and be wrong than to be depressed for years because I am afraid of the outcome.

Will there be a happy ending
When all of this is through?
Or will I wish I had given up
and found something else to do?

Will there be a happy ending?
Will I laugh, instead of cry?
Turn lemons into lemonade?
Can I make it if I try?

There springs that hope eternal
That things will turn out right.
Please don't confuse me with the facts.
Cause then I'd lose the fight.

One day, I'll say, it's worth it all,
The troubles I have seen.
Or do I have the wrong perspective?
Am I allowed to dream?
Will I find the pot of gold?
Does the rainbow follow rain?
Or will I open up my eyes to see
That my optimism was in vain?

I know that happy ever after
Only comes in fairy tales.
But I can't shake the feeling
That all will turn out well.

So you may think that I'm a fool,
But I must stop pretending.
I can't accept the doom and gloom.
I will have my happy ending.

Claudreen Jackson

A LOVE SO PURE

This is the poem that I never thought I would write.

A love so pure,
That I am sure
It's coming straight from God.
This kind of love
Comes down from above
And right into my heart.

Your smiling eyes
Were a big surprise.
That I thought I'd never see.
So who knew that one day you
Would be smiling down at me?

How could I guess
That I'd be blessed
For taking care of you?
You've taught me
A lot of things
About how love can be true.

I never thought
The day would come
When you'd be teaching me.
But, now I'm sure
That when love is pure
It's unconditionally.

Claudreen Jackson

HE HOLDS THE FUTURE...

Sometimes the future can be frightening, but that's when it is important to have faith. If you already know the outcome will be good you don't need Faith. Dr. Norman Vincent Peale said that the only force more powerful than fear is Faith. When I am afraid for PJ's future, I try to remember this...

When storms are raging 'round me
And I'm drowning in quicksand,
And unhappy things are happening,
Things that I don't understand,
When I don't know what else to do,
I'll just do what I can.
Because He who holds the Future
He also holds my hand.

I'll believe that God is with me
Every step of the way.
If He brought me to it
He'll bring me through it,
So in His care I'll stay.
And I will face my future
According to His plan.
He who holds the Future
Also holds my hand.

THANKS A LOT

This poem is for everyone who reads this book.

How do you say, well, thanks a lot?
When words just seem so small?
One word can't tell you how I feel.
One word can't say it all.

I appreciate your time and effort,
And your interest, too.
I could not do it by myself.
I surely needed you.

I would gladly give you recompense
For what you have been worth,
But that much gold cannot be found
In all the vaults on earth.

So, I'll simply say, I thank you,
And send my love to you.
With good wishes for your future.
We've helped each other through.

Claudreen Jackson

*Poems From
Pervis Jackson, Sr.*

PEOPLE, TOO

Handicapped children are people too
Just as human as me and you
Sent to us from God above.
It's up to us to give them love.

Some can't run and some can't walk.
Some can't see and some can't talk.
But there are lots of things
That they can do.
Some, even better than me and you.
So, let's come together
In our point of view.

Give them a chance
Your life to enhance
Give them your best
They've passed the test.
Heed the call,
Don't let our children fall.

Their inspiration can overcome doubt.
Let's give them something to cheer about.
Take a stand throughout the land
To lend a hand to your fellow man.

PJ

People look at you like you don't exist,
But you have a lot of qualities
That the people miss.

You're different from others in so many ways.
There are a lot of things that you want to say
So, I'll be your voice come what may.

You look to us for guidance and truth
I'll try to do my best for you.

I'll do for you whatever I can,
You are always part of my plan.
The bottom line is I'm your old man.
And I don't care what people say
I'm going to love you anyway.

Pervis

11

Chapter Eleven

Laughs Inspired By Autism

Laughs
Inspired By
Autism

By Claudreen Jackson

Inspired By Autism   Claudreen Jackson

PJ has a lot of energy...
He climbs on everything...

I try to protect him and make
sure he doesn't hurt himself...

PJ don't jump...
You might hurt yourself...

Well at least he
didn't
hurt himself...

...Ow...

PJ is learning new words every day...

Now he can ask for what he wants...

Shultz...

Shutlz...

Shutlz...

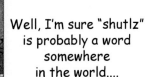

Shultz!

Shultz!

Well, I'm sure "shutlz" is probably a word somewhere in the world....

PJ is starting to talk...

Now he can name some of the things he sees...

Quarter ... Quarter...

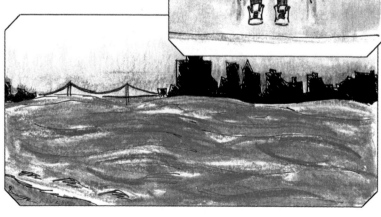

Well "quarter" kind of rhymes with "water"

PJ is learning
to dress himself.

He can even choose
his own clothes.

Time to put on
some clothes, PJ.

Well...
He is learning
to "dress" himself.

Inspired By Autism   Claudreen Jackson

PJ is really learning self control...

I can take him out now without worrying about one of his *"moments"*...

PJ can even pick out personal items he wants and needs...

Well ...
at least personal items...

PJ is learning how to follow simple instructions.

We can even cook together sometimes...

One day I asked PJ to get some flour because we were making a cake...

I did say simple instructions...
And the flowers did smell good...

PJ learned another
new word today!

He said mouth!
Now he understands
what mouth means.

Well...
Mouse and Mouth
both start
with a "M."

PJ has special skills
and talents.
He can cook his own
french fries and bacon.
He also has a great voice
and loves to sing and dance.

He was invited to share
his talents by singing with
his sister at a benefit
for autism....

Well ... He didn't feel much like sharing that day...

135

We Want To Hear From You

You hear a lot about the autism spectrum, but you don't hear much about our end of the spectrum, parents of adult children with autism. Our children came along before all the intervention treatments that are available now (if you can afford them). We would like to hear from parents of adults with autism, or the adults themselves. What happened to them after their education was over. Are they living independently? In group homes? Still living with their parents (PJ is)?

For autistic adults who are still living with their parents, are they employed? Are they in a day program (PJ is)? How much respite is available for parents? How long will they continue to live with parents? In my case, I am not sure.

You can reach me by:

- E-mail at jacksonclaudreen@sbcglobal.net
- Claudreen Jackson PO Box 04422 Detroit, MI 48204

About the Author

Claudreen Jackson is a retired special education teacher from Detroit Public Schools who taught students with learning disabilities. Among other honors, she was twice a finalist for Michigan Teacher of the Year as well as twice a finalist for Television Station WDIV's Outstanding Teacher Award.

Before teaching, Claudreen was an advocate on a state wide level for people with disabilities in the State of Michigan. She served on many committees, including appointments by both Governors Blanchard and Engler to their advisory council, The Michigan State Planning Council for Developmental Disabilities. She was a member of the State Board of Directors of the Michigan Society for Autistic Citizens (now Autism Society of Michigan). She served as the president of the Wayne county Chapter and as a member of the United Foundation Speakers' Bureau. During this time in 1987 and 1988 she produced and hosted an award winning cable television show about autism, "My Piece of the Puzzle."

She is the parent of four children, the youngest is handicapped by autism and is the motivation for her advocacy efforts.

Claudreen was married to Pervis Jackson, a founding member of the Spinners singing group, one of the original Motown groups. Pervis died in August, 2008, but not before mentoring and inspiring Claudreen in her writing endeavors.

Claudreen had many articles published in various disability magazines during the 1980s. Her latest publications include "Plus Magazine" (one of the Guidepost Publications), "The Michigan Chronicle" and comments in the "Detroit Free Press." She also has an article in the Red Hatters Book, *Sassy, Classy and Still Sparkling*.

She can be reached via her website www.claudreenjackson.com or by e-mail at jacksonclaudreen@sbcglobal.net.

Help When You Need It Most

Damon's House Incorporated
(313) 245-273
11900 E. McNichols Rd.
Detroit, MI 48205
damonhouse@aol.com
http://damonshouse.org/

Damon's House Mission

It is the mission of Damon's House, Inc. to bridge the gap of understanding that allows us to accept those persons who are least understood in society. i.e. persons with autism.

It is our mission to offer awareness about the challenges and obstacles a person with autism must face in coping with the issues of social/recreation interaction.

It is our mission to develop in persons with autism those coping skills needed to penetrate the walls of isolation that surrounds persons with autism.

Burger School for Students with Autism
30922 Beechwood
Garden City, MI 48135
Phone: (734) 762-8420

Autism Society of America
7910 Woodmont Ave., Suite 300
Bethesda, MD 20814-3015
www.autism-society.org

(800) 3autism x 150
(301) 657-0881

Judson Center
4410 W. Thirteen Mile Road
Royal Oak, MI 48073-6515
www.judsoncenter.org
(248) 549-4339

Detroit Institute for Children
Main Office - Detroit
5447 Woodward
Detroit, MI 48202
www.detroitchildren.org
(313) 832-1100
(313) 832-6263

Resource Page

To order additional copies of *Inspired By Autism* or to find out about other books by Claudreen Jackson or Zoë Life Publishing, please visit our website at www.zoelifepub.com.

For more information about Claudreen Jackson, *Inspired By Autism* or the "Pervis Jackson, Jr. Autism Foundation," offering a spoonful of comfort to parents of children with disabilities, visit her website at www.pjjraf.org.

Quantity discounts are available directly from the publisher for bulk orders of *Inspired by Autism*.

Zoë Life Publishing
P.O. Box 871066
Canton, MI 48187
(877) 841-3400
outreach@zoelifepub.com